Foreword

by Kidder Smith

If you have a minute, open this book at random. It's holographic, any place will do.

And if you have an hour, or a lifetime, open these as well—a hologram becomes only stronger the more we see of it.

Good. But this book works in the other direction: the more we see of it, the more we see in the way that it sees. And then the more our present sight reveals itself as God's own seeing eye, until there is only seeing, a bringing forth of this world. That seeing is the act of love. And this love is only Mystery.

Still, there is form. And when we are still, forms frolic, making and unmaking themselves, shifting like anything, a delicacy so precise that at once it shatters into another specificity, form becoming form becoming form, beyond intelligence, and never moving at all.

Amidst this joy and sorrow, there can be only one regret: neglecting form's invitation to the sighting of love. Oh, but it is here, again, and who could say no to this kind of loving?

Kidder Smith
Professor of Asian Studies and History,
Emeritus—Bowdoin
The Art of War: A New Translation,
with essays and commentary; collaborative
work by Denma Translation Group;
http://www.bowdoin.edu/faculty/k/kidder/

Foreword

by M. Young

In these pages Traktung Yeshe Dorje speaks spontaneously to the heart of the matter in a way that is balm for my heart, which longs for the sound of my guru's voice, now almost two years since his passing from the physical body in *mahasamadhi*. Traktung and my guru, Lee Lozowick, were—and are—friends. In this lifetime they spent only a few days together in each other's company, but they are close kin of the spirit—fierce lovers of truth in all its raw glory.

When they first met, it was Traktung's impeccable respect for the immutable laws of spiritual work and protocol that gave Lee great enjoyment and kindled the first sparks of good company between them. Traktung's direct, fearless way of self-immolation through searing declaration—which deftly skewered any lingering attachment to self-image—rang like the bells of freedom to Lee, who had mastered the fine art of self-deconstruction. But perhaps most of all, it was stories of Traktung's relationship with his own guru, the revered vajra master Thinley Norbu Rinpoche, that resonated with Lee's life-long relationship with his master, Yogi Ramsuratkumar.

Traktung's gift as wordsmith was another dimension of their friendship that brought great delight to Lee in the last year of his life. With glee and satisfaction, Lee read his friend's letters aloud to his own students, saying, "This guy can write! A man after my own heart! Listen to this…" It was Traktung's wish for Lee to write a foreword for this book, as Traktung has often done for Lee's books. Oh, how Lee would have enjoyed this book!

When Traktung writes, "I am hiding amidst everyone. I have made the walls of my retreat hut from the fabric of appearance, hidden my mind in the emptiness of space and safeguarded my love in the guise of all beings," again I hear that uncanny resonance with my guru, who was wily and even heretical in the ways of hiding his innate knowledge of divinity within the ordinary. Lee lived a deep intimacy with the reality of being utterly alone, "Satisfied with the joy in the cracks between my sorrows, not counting on a future of illusory tomorrows," as he once wrote in a song.

Traktung calls to us from the wilderness of solitary being in phrases like "conceptuality's bewilderment," which speak to the predicament of our identification with concept, idea, opinion, all born of the separate self. What concept of the mind is not ultimately bewildered and bewildering, leading us deeper into the tangled backwoods of illusion, in fact the very hell we inhabit? The clarity with which this is seen brings its opposite into view— that which is madly, wildly Real, the volcano, the tsunami, the burning bush, the eyes of a newborn or the one who dwells at the threshold of death, the Godwave of grace and mercy that forges faith on the red hot coals of experience.

In the words of this book there is an exquisite, often tender mood of reality as it is that may be consumed and digested. Ultimately, these are dangerous words, for if we do not feast freely—happily reduced to nothing and therefore rendered into the Real—then they have the potency to simply infect us, to saturate us with the writer's view so that we are slowly steeped in a great necessity for transformation, fruitful emptiness, and its revelation of infinite possibility. This is the writer's offering: to take us into the intimate moment of his direct perception—what the Bauls call "bartaman," a direct experience of the Supreme Reality.

This mysterious capacity for *sahaja* or union with the primordial nature arising in this present moment is shared by Traktung and Lee, who both carry the gift of transmission through the written word. Although Lee cannot sit down, pick up pen and paper, and write a foreword for this book, resonance endures beyond the appearance of death. And so, in the name of my guru, this invitation is offered to the courageous reader to come, freely eat, drink, digest and be remade in the miracle that belongs to all.

M. Young
Ramji, Ferme de Jutreau
France
July 19, 2012

100 days

1.

For the higher we soar in contemplation the more limited
become our expressions of that which is purely
intelligible; even as now, when plunging into the
Darkness that is above the intellect, we pass not merely
into brevity of speech, but even into absolute silence of
thoughts and of words.

—Pseudo-Dionysius

Early dawn. Walking across the field the light, in gold and topaz, pervades the world with a tender affection. Mind, silent and still, touches appearance with tremendous fondness. A bird sitting on a branch in the autumn cold ruffles its feathers in an attempt to create warmth. The branch, dark black and flecked with green lichen, forms a pattern against the blue sky. A tiny vine twists and turns across the tree's limbs like secret Taoist script. Bird, branch, tangle of vine divulge an unutterable intimacy within mystery . . . and joy surges within the mind's silence.

Mind settled in silence imbues the world with beauty and the world's color, shape and form evoke an ever-deeper silence within mind's expanse. Mind and world, like the banks of a river and its water, hold and flow within each other. When mind is free from contradictions and chaos then perception becomes meditation divulging the unity of unborn divinity in the act of living. This unity has no inner and outer but exists in the luminous conversation of perceiving. It is a country for appearance, a land where eye to form is only love.

Suddenly a bird explodes from a tangled thicket of tall grass. Its flurry of feather and motion breaks across the stillness of both mind and sky. The body, alert and still, perceives with-in-as wholeness. Mind, feeling, flesh, each of these is an organ of perception that embodies, enworlds mysterious wholeness. In the silence of meditation mind does not go out to meet what is seen, nor does the appearance enter the mind; both are held within impenetrable mystery. Within the dimension where stillness and motion are single the flight of the bird exists as delight.

When the body and mind are harnessed by the habits of confusion then suffering shackles perception and, in the place of intimacy and joy, alienation and angst thrive. The spiritual path frees energy consumed by mechanical habit, the energy needed to break the shackles of delusion. In ancient China this unlearning of delusion was called *zuanxue*, "dark learning" wherein conceptuality's bewilderment is unmade, unknown.

The bird is flying back to its nest now, a small twig in its mouth. Its movement is inside of me, I am inside of it . . . sky, motion, bird, perceiving, twig, pattern of dark branch—all so beautiful that its wonder is beyond imagination.

2.

I am hiding amidst everyone. I have made the walls of my
retreat hut from the fabric of appearance, hidden my mind in the
emptiness of space and safeguarded my love in the guise of all
beings.

∾

Smaller than the smallest house of time (the present), smaller
than the smallest place of space (the "here"), vaster than the
manifest totality, is the mysterious reality. No "others," no "self," no
"beings," no "Buddhas," no "past," no "future," no "present"—only
mystery .... the delicacy of AwarenessAppearance without
fragmentation.

∾

Here in my little hut I am the richest man in the world. There
is a dead vine on the fence, killed by winter, and a broken pot at
the bottom of the stair. If I had something I would give it away.
Having nothing I give that away too.

3.

Hamburg, Germany: People filled the room to overflowing. It was a Karma Kagyu temple, filled with the substance of tradition; statues, images of Lamas, gurus, and the seating reflected the politics of hierarchy with all its fretful hopes and fears. All of this can serve to numb the mind or it can serve to turn the mind away from coarseness with longing for the subtle. The hindering force of such trappings is only relevant to a mind that has not yet become earnest and sincere in its exploration.

People had heard that a western-born tulku, an enlightened Lama, would be speaking. Some had come to listen, others to challenge. Some had come with spiritual expectations of lineage, others in hope of hearing something fresh, different. For a time we sat together in the possibility offered by silence. There is, in silence, a chance of communion beyond notions "self and other," an introduction to divine mystery. The communication of words, more often than not, is the breakdown of communion. This body mind has been drowned in the silence and fullness of wisdom. It longs for the possibility of sharing that is communion; it thirsts for it as the pregnant rain cloud seeks to shower on the parched earth.

A middle-aged man sat in the back. He had very red hair and a look of aggressive anticipation. His lounging posture, like a sack of potatoes, made clear his contempt for structure or form. His aggressive gaze made clear that he had come with his challenge well planned. With the presumed power of cleverness his question was designed to catch the speaker in some contradiction of dogma and tradition. His intention was to upstage the stodginess of tradition with the cleverness of modernity. The response of deep of silence unraveled the question; its intention was felt as shallowness, and the questioner giggled nervously.

When the mind is made sensitive to the reality of truth, beauty and goodness then games based in the silliness of authority, dogma, dominance, disappear. The path requires an earnestness that simply has no time or place for such superficiality. Without such sincerity the path devolves into tawdry foolishness. Carl Jung's statement "Where there is the will to power there is no love and where there is love there is no will to power" is very true.

Another person asked what the speaker thought of a certain guru of this or that tradition. Sitting for a moment with the question in silence, affection seemed to fill one. Out of affection the answer urged the questioner to forsake such curiosities and not let the meeting devolve to the level of *People Magazine* spirituality.

Within silence the speaker began to sing a small prayer. Words can form sounds that disclose humanity's shallowness or make known the possibility of great depths. A woman in the back cried gentle tears, her mind moved by a mysterious and spontaneous love.

4.

We are too late for gods and too
early for Being. Being's poem, just
begun, is man.
            —Heidegger, *Poetry, Language and Thought*

and even flesh becomes poetry) Appearance announces
but birth
            is mere rumor.

Solidity of curve and line do not convict. They fall short
of reasonable doubt, their evidence not unquestionable.
Eye-witness accounts reveal confusions and are deemed
"not reliable."

Play entices, intending, intimating, direction currents
recursive eddies and
vectors   whose

Closed loop systems turn out to have back door exits.
The path of moonlight.   (And, what's more,
            dawn light breaks the edge of mind

5.

For many years not a day would pass in which I didn't
feel intense fear at the thought of my life slipping away
before I realized its deepest meaning. One day I jotted
down a bit of advice from me to myself about this illness that cures.

Things to be kept together. Things to be kept apart.

Emptiness' open space and luminosity's clarity,
these are two things that should not be kept apart.

Mind's luminosity and deity's form,
These are two things that should not be kept apart.

The appearance of beings and spontaneous compassion,
these are two things that should not be kept apart.

The practice of dharma and public display,
these are two things that should be kept apart.

Speculative talk and one's precious time,
These are two things that should be kept apart.

The mind's intrinsic dignity and the eight worldly concerns,
these are two things that should be kept apart.

The world's appearance and the celestial palace,
these are two things that should not be kept apart.

The sun and the moon as seat for the deity,
these are two things that should not be kept apart.

One's every breath and the deity's recitation,
these are two things that should not be kept apart.

The waning days of our lives and problematic companions,
these are two things that should be kept apart.

Our every breath and negative gossips,
these are two things that should be kept apart.

Our mind's freedom and kowtowing to others,
these are two things that should be kept apart.

One's every moment and the inner warmth,
these are two things that should be kept together.

The precious bindu and our own body
these are two things that should be kept together.

The mind's great bliss and the expanse of space,
these are two things that should be kept together.

A leaky faucet and an expensive mansion,
these are two things that should be kept apart.

Jungle tigers and sheep in a pen,
these are two things that should be kept apart.

Ordinary desiring and the great third conduct,
these are two things that should be kept apart.

Primordial purity and easeful spontaneity,
these are two things that should not be kept apart.

All appearance and empty awareness,
these are two things that should not be kept apart.

All phenomena and complete exhaustion,
these are two things that should not be kept apart.

A high view but low actions,
this brings shame upon a yogi.

Fancy words but no realization,
this signals the old age of a lineage.

Buddha's dharma and politics,
This means the nail has been driven in the coffin.

If you are scared that death's appointment with your life might come before you have understood the meaning of Buddha's words then shun all politics and the eight worldly concerns, embrace the lineage of practice, cultivate unwavering faith in the Guru and utter sincerity. With these there is no way to fail.

6.

This room where we live is only mystery; presencing
and love. And yet two paths spin out from possibility—
1. manifest love, 2. confusion.
Without beginning or end   without defining
forever   in this freedom place, the choice is ours.

Form and emptiness gone to ease in wisdom offer
themselves one to the other without hesitation—the
single act of love.

Auto Commentary: This love makes and unmakes me. This
"me" only body, flesh, world, all appearance. Wisdom knows all
appearance as the only body there is and it knows this as Love.
Body, the presencing of emptiness, wave crested . . . about to fall.
When the "I" and "me" made of mind dissolve in the native bliss
then wisdom undermines contrivance and joy of heart is known.
Joy of heart is lived as incarnation in-of-as Love.

What is this meaty act of appearing, seeming so solid yet empty of
defining substance? The act of confusion or the response of love—
these are the only choices. The body of life, single body, stars, sofa,
planets, rusted-out car in a gully, crying child in the Walmart aisle,
jet stream dip, giant squid. God showed Jonah a whale, a sunrise,
the mystery of appearing and disappearing and Jonah's life was
right again. Jonah's mind went where no mind goes—the silent
wisdom. His body was born anew in bliss despite the vagaries of
circumstance.

Mind, gone to emptiness in wisdom, has no location, no form,
no substance, no characteristic, no attributes, no color, no shape,
no point of view, no high or low, no bondage or freedom. Heart,

gone to brightness in love, knows every form as the only body, its beloved. Beloved as every being, every rock, every person, every individual, every act, every turn and angle of temporariness. Body, surrendered into the discipline of love, becomes the enactment of primordial longing—the longing of love to love.

In truth there is no furtive inner "I." No "me" or "mine." But outwardly the delight-appearance of life itself waxes and wanes, flows, spins in currents and eddies of wisdom and emptiness. This love manifests in realms and beings but is not mere nature—that machine of eating and being eaten. This movement of delight manifests in every interaction—but it is not mere relationship, that mechanism of fretful searching. Instead it is the always present deep of the ocean on which the waves rise and fall. It is the womb space of the sky, spacious and vast, unmoved by the changing weather.

And now, mind gone silent, form and emptiness embrace.

7.

We both step and do not step in the same rivers. We are and are not.

—Heraclitus

Once upon a time Aristotle, that sage founder of our tradition of reason and logic, was walking down the beach. It was a crisp clear day and the ocean waves were perfectly still leaving the surface of the water like a mirror. Further down the beach Aristotle could see an unusual activity taking place; a man was running to the water's edge, bending down and then running a short way back up the beach toward the sand.

After some time Aristotle came close enough to recognize the figure, Heraclitus, that enigmatic figure who many called The Obscure and others called The Riddler. Now Aristotle's mind became full of irritating thoughts as he recalled the words of Heraclitus' philosophy such as "flow, transformation, hidden harmony." There was no harmony between his system and the system of this man who hid his confusions behind enigmatic meaninglessness, mystic mumbo jumbo.

Coming closer Aristotle called out, "Hello there good man, what are you doing?" Heraclitus stopped his frenetic activity and answered, "Ah, yes, I am using this spoon for a grand project. I have dug this small hole here in the sand and I am taking the water from the ocean and filling the hole. Let me show you." Thus said, Heraclitus ran back down to the water, filled the spoon, ran back and poured the contents into the hole. Aristotle, now standing by the hole, looked down and saw the water sink into the sand leaving the hole empty again. "You are a fool!" exclaimed Aristotle, "Look at the vast ocean, look at your tiny hole, you can not fit the ocean into the hole. And, as soon as you pour the water in it rushes back out again. Look! The hole is empty!"

Heraclitus did not seem disturbed by this, in fact, he laughed out loud. "Yes, yes, you speak truly. But, my dear Aristotle, if this makes me a fool then what are you? Look how vast the universe is and how small your head. You will never fit the mystery of this universe into your small box of reason. Death will come and your head will also be empty."

Jean Piaget discovered that a child develops their capacity for knowing organically along with age and brain development. The brain is one organ of knowledge, there are others. Subtle capacities for knowing truth, beauty, love, enlightenment abide within the human being. There are human stages of growth just as for children but these higher stages require conscious participation. They are the inner import of the spiritual path. When a human being matures beyond satisfaction with the shallow consolation of a society based on partial wisdom then they will seek the way . . . and it is there.

8.

A blossom falls from the pear tree and, in its
        f a
           l
             l ing,
the pear appears. This body, atoms spun from a thread
of mystery, and in its
                 spinning the guest appears.
                     Face all radiance,
                     a country for appearance.

for unborn mystery's love)
a sun, a moon, a staircase of light, all of these dwell
within the body. a seeming birth, a seeming death,   and
in between a single pause. This life,   a trembling
moment reconciled,
                in ...... (there is no word

The seed dies becoming the sprout; that's almost cliché.
But have you considered that the boy gives birth to the
father? Between birth and death there is a breath and a
breath within the breath and within that second subtle
breath stars find their fuel, whole galaxies spin
             out
                beyond, the numbers one or
two,   beyond
the boundaries of past and present tense.

In the clay pot body's dying there is the
           fa
           l
           l
              ing of a pear blossom.

9.

We are more than merely perceptual beings, we are Perceptual Being. We are perceiving organisms, the whole body and life as the act of perceiving and so our perceiving and our living are single like the banks of a river and the river—but which is which or both and neither. Within and without, perceiving and perceived, nature and nurture are all co-emergent and so perfectly interdependent that there is no separation. They are beyond the numbers two or one. The human being is a specific limit of perception.

The strata of perception called, "human being" is an ever-shifting middle layer of possibility. Below there is the deep ocean of the unconscious and above there is the vast sky, a mystery of unborn awareness. Human consciousness resides between these two in a ceaseless conversation with itself . Carl Jung discovered that archetypal symbols bubble up from the unconscious and act as transformative forces in the human psyche. It is also true that transformative symbols bubble down from the meta-conscious awareness to act as transformative symbols in human psyche as well.

Below and above are fluid realms of dynamically alive symbol. This human realm is also a fluid realm of living symbol made to seem solid by the cement of concepts, identification, habits. Reality habit. The realm, the beings therein, our "selves" are perceptual habits constructed and deconstructed by birth, living and death.

Mind, body and feeling act as a single whole, a bubble of perception, floating through/in/as a sea of possibility. Worlds of definition are built by the mind, lived in by body, aesthetically known in feeling. The mytho-poetics of language act as the banks of a river, shaping and being shaped by perception. Spiritual life, in its deepest form, is a psycho-physical adventurism. It is a practical phenomenology that traverses the domains of "Being"—the above, the below, the middle, until it finds itself in a freedom beyond, yet intimately interconnected with, the patterning function itself.

Tantricas are masters of living symbol, of the dynamic fluid intensity of patterning and perception. They learn to deconstruct the rigidity of perceptual patterning through systems of psycho-physical gymnastics and discover the wisdom bliss that is the dimension from which all perception and pattern arise. From this they move even beyond into the perfect unborn wisdom mystery.

Tantricas take in the below and the above, bring them into the middle ground, and work them with such depth and discipline that they dissolve the borderlines. They use experience to understand experiencing. They discover the space in which experience takes place. Fullness of wisdom is beyond experience. Until one can distinguish between wisdom and experience one will be lost in identification with shifting appearances and spiritual life remains immature.

10.

In this worldly marketplace I am an aimless drifter
having no value. I have nothing to sell, no need for a
shopping cart app. To be frank I am a bum;
sit here by my side and I'll share my homemade brew.

First take the pot of the body,
and the juice of precious human birth.
Add the yeast of the guru's word
mix and let simmer. You'll see bubbling in no time.

Next, in the belly, light the fire of great bliss,
fan it with the winds of diligence
till melting and dripping begin in earnest.
Harnessing exaltation, you'll see strong liquor in no time.

Blazing and dripping, descent and return,
the fierce inner fire , the yogi's delight!
Drunk on the fourth joy's intoxication,
too drunk for concepts—you'll see results in no time!

The lotus, the vajra, the mortar, the pestle,
emptiness bliss without a distinction.
Find the body to be a garden of treasures
and you'll know great freedom in no time!

The clothes of illusion dress the nothingness state,
the body appears but is mind's own façade.
Like the empty reflection of emptiness shining,
reality's habit will see death in no time.

In the dark of deep sleep ignorance rules,
but if you draw in clear light then Nothingness shines.

Rising at dawn from the great Dharmakaya,
you'll find liberation in appearance, right where you are.

Precious Guru, Indestructible Wisdom Bliss, within the
dimension without birth or movement, AwarenessAppearance
is an unceasing delight. On a windy night in the
open field of Blazing Jewel Mountain I, a useless
vagrant, offered this song to the charming yoginis who
practice the two stages of generation and completion.
May the self-manifest mountain of wisdom awareness
remain our sole homeland forever.

11.

The stars shone brightly in the dark blue of the early morning sky and a sliver of moon was cradled in openness. Waking before dawn the mind comes alive in Silence allowing perception to be unmodified by concept and, thus, a vast freedom is known. Standing on the small porch of the hut there was the sound of a possum scurrying in the tall grass towards the wood. Anxiety over life, pain, hurt, is natural to the embodied creature, and this anxiety spills over the mind and psyche as well. Is it possible for the body to remain sensitive to danger but for the mind to be free from psychological holding to hurts? Can one be free from anxiety and its attendant fear?

When the mind is in order, without contradictions or chaos, then one moves from deep sleep to waking with the clarity of fresh awareness—and in this clarity one is able to witness the arising of mind's functioning. A deep mystery, whose functioning is awareness, is able to witness the birth of consciousness with its structuring process, its modification and finally its concepts and "self." In this simple awareness, prior to consciousness, there is no identity only a luminous expanse suffused by affection. There is a knowing without a knower and this creates a space that is beyond the feeling of threat. The brain then can rest beyond anxiety and is nurtured and made sensitive to the connection between mind's functioning and its deep unborn state. Appearances known in this way are felt as a continuum of meaning and sanctity arising inseparable from unborn wisdom.

So much of our society is built on the structure of psychological fear and frantic attempts to find security in the face of this fear. Love becomes wounded by the inherent frailty of identity and grasping to pleasure, security, takes Love's place. Joy is lost and aggressive seeking after a succession of fun moments takes its place. Silence, peace of mind, is lost and in its place the need for excitement becomes addictive. Vulnerability is lost, and so alienation grows and greed for objects and possessions replaces tenderness.

The force of psychological memory can be washed away but not by strategies born of the same mechanism that gave birth to fear. These memory wounds are cleansed in a profound blessedness that is natural to the mind when mind is in touch with its own depths. Meditation, the unity of the silent mind and appearance, opens the doorway to this natural sacredness.

Standing on the porch, the body was free from all memory, even the memory of being. The mystery of the vast open sky met the mystery of the body like water poured into water. Between eye and star there was no distance. In this wholeness, unfractured by the past, there was the coming of Love.

12.

Love was never else where and when—I—   stopped
calling everything that was not love by the name of love,
there was love right where it had been all along.

The lover of Love owns nothing and even that he longs to give
away. The intellectual tries to figure out the percentage
of profit on this bargain. The percentage is not good.

In a secret place hidden before mind, is a space without
Measure—a perfect right angle to appearance yet embracing is .....
..... bright with birthlessness it is pure presence.
The body of realization is a pin-prick of light shining
through the dark.

Devotees burn the world to ash in that brightness and in
the remains they find a jewel. Even giving this away
they sing a song of the Empty Heart.

All of it makes for bad business. All of it makes for
unborn joy.
                This is the path of all loss, no gain—who
        wants that? Who wants to give up the great
        mantra "What about me?" Love is radiance,
        outward directive non-self-referencing
        brightness. Self concern is the occluded dullness
        of love.

Love is not sense making. Love is not relationship.
Relationship is a subset of love. Logic is a subset of
knowing. Appearance is a subset of awareness.
Relationship as Love is all give with no center from
which "give" is given.

13.

There is renewal only with the cessation of the centre; then rebirth is not continuity; then death is as life, a renewal from moment to moment.
—Krishnamurti

"The raw ore is removed from the earth and sized into pieces that range from 0.5 to 1.5 inches ..."
—*Journal of Steel*

To know is to un-notice,
and we are made by our knowings.
Made solid, sure,

wrong.

"Alloying element: Any metallic element added during the melting of steel or aluminum for the purpose of increasing corrosion resistance, hardness, or strength." — *Journal of Steel*

Briquettes of knowledge, describe, define, parameters of allowable motion. Silence un-knows. Love
un-thinks, but
too late.

"Camber Tolerances 1: Camber is the deviation from edge straightness. Maximum allowable tolerance of this deviation of a side edge from a straight line are defined in ASTM Standards1.
—*Journal of Steel*

Others are inconvenient ... Inconvenient deviations from edge straightness.

"Maximum
allowable tolerance
demands increase. Cold
reduction doubles length.
Contract sales control price
fluctuation." Dinner is
eaten out. —*Journal of Steel*

Can you un-see, un-know, a leaf, a friend, a life?

"Descaling 1: The process of removing scale from
the surface of steel. Scale forms most readily when
the steel is hot by union of oxygen with iron.
Common methods are: (1) crack the scale by use
of roughened rolls and remove by a forceful water
spray, (2) throw salt or wet sand or wet burlap on
the steel just previous to its passage through the
rolls." —*Journal of Steel*

14.

When mind is free from past, free from future, free even from the concept "Now," there is a deep and infinite Silence whose nature is radiant beauty. In this silence the senses open like a flower embracing appearance—and yet paradoxically neither senses nor appearance move in any way. Lover and Beloved embrace beyond two or one. Every perception becomes "guru" and Silence itself offers up the deepest instructions.

∽

When Silence overwhelms appearance this body becomes Love. Every artist expresses the "meaning state" of themselves and their culture. All art is expression of "meaning states" in non-linear methods. In truth all urge to art is the expression of a "meaning saturated state," the Total Buddha Nature attempting to communicate. In a Buddha this urge becomes perfect manifestation. Be moved by this urge.

∽

The human being is a perceptual event unfolding across the stage of space and time and paradoxically space and time are part of the unfolding. The entangled play of perceiver and perceived unfolds the dynamic intimacy of perception. All of this is the luminous potency of pure mystery. Mystery's capacity for knowingness is mistaken as subjectivity and mystery's luminous display is mistaken for "existent" objects and the tension between these creates the feeling Being. But, in truth, subject and object are not two and not even One.

15.

If your robe is white but your heart is black—
What then, yogi?

If your hair is long but your compassion short—
What then, yogi?

If your ornaments jangle but so does your mind—
What then, yogi?

If your posture is perfect but your heart is crooked—
What then, yogi?

If your status is high but your qualities low—
What then, yogi?

If the monk dyes his robe red but his heart is not dyed
in the color of love, what then? If the yogi wears a
simple robe of white but his mind, stained with
grasping, is drenched in the color of death—what then?

He is a real yogi who can sit upon a stainless lotus
without roots, whose heart resounds with silence, who
eats the pulse and rhythm of Being for breakfast and
who wears the body of illusions. Standing outside all
concerns, an ornament of Love, he is at rest in the
midst of all actions.

16.

The dark night mist moved through the woods in patterns of hiding and revealing. The body, alive with wonder, felt the urge toward creation—a longing to incarnate beauty, truth, goodness in forms of sound, light, color, movement. Art as communication of wonder—the conversation between humanity and the divine, is deeply rooted in the very cells of the body.

A liberation theology of art could help to undo the effects of this deadening time when art has been co-opted by the shabbiness of commercialism and the shallowness of fashion. An aesthetics of sublimity is needed. In every moment beauty surges forth from-in-as-of the unborn wisdom mind disrupting the status quo of mediocre conceptuality. The self-liberating dynamic of wisdom bliss functions through beauty, playfulness and creativity. It invites, seduces and provokes beings out from the mediocrity of subject/object's dulled perception.

Those who engage the work of transforming narrow and constricted habits of mind, feeling and body become sensitive to the nourishment inherent in true art. While the essence of wisdom mind is an expanse free from any quality, characteristic or attribute its nature is luminous, communicative and dynamic. It is a communicative thrust inherent within truth whose energy becomes the ceaseless magical display of appearances. In the human being the urge toward art is an urge toward rediscovery of this expanse of beauty as communication.

The essence of unborn wisdom is a meaning saturated field. The nature of awareness is bright with love, which is felt as infinite being and bliss. It is replete with the dynamic radiance of innumerable sublime qualities. The energy of awareness becomes the ever-shifting play of that light as presencing, as appearing. Art, in its most profound form, is the communication of meaning saturation inherent in perception itself. Art is always communication; sadly, more often than not, it is the communication of alienation's constricted neurosis.

Just as there can not be realization of truth without manifestation of love there can not be the manifestation of truth or love without participation in beauty and its embodiment and enworldment.

17.

Non-dual dualism.

The longing of love becomes the stuff of appearing, god's whisper. Since the very beginning of *No Time At All* the vast expanse has presenced its ownmost mystery as that intensity extensity, expanse and tiny-ness, of time and space.

Bright knowing shines as natural activity across the expanse of mystery. It is better to say that the expanse *is* itself the shining. Mystery shines and its shining creates space across which that shining happens. First there was no "space" and then the nature of dark mystery shone radiant across a space. Space that came into being through the action of shining.

Space prior to any dimensionality shimmers as the frolic of pristine awareness. The shimmering sets up the play of pattern, dimensions, realms, beings and the knowing of these. Awareness knows the patterns which are only the patterning of awareness' own shimmering that is only the radiance of dark mystery's own unutterableness . . . and so knowing and known come into being.

Like a shooting star a single drop of knowing falls—creating now the vertical and horizontal dimensions of space. And the falling creates a dimension known as duration. Falling from the sky of mind the world is the becoming of being and luminous emptiness is known as-is every where and when.

A mystery speaks without lips or tongue. There is the whisper, "I love you." It falls, like the sound of bells, into-as the face of all existence. This simple urge, love, mystery's bright, spreads across the sky with dawn's rays and the rice bag body appears. It lives— like a puppet on the strings of love.

Body forgets the divine origin and luminous secret of flesh and form and so finds "itself" here and now. Here and now, the illusions of space and time, clothe love's impulse, but in dark forgetting are forgotten, and so the fretful search begins.

The search seeks across space and time for the secret of what is not space and time. It looks in the only time and place it knows and so falls short since the secret is not in place or time and so .... so much suffering frustration. And yet, secret is born and wed to flesh, to happy urge. In hidden place the placelessness, the heart within the heart, the breath within the breath. Animated in everything and every when where and why, the subtle insistence. The dull and dim of fretful mind can unbecome and know in brightness once again.

18.

Gnosemic nuclei: 1

hildegard understood god's flirtation,
green's sensuous disclosure,
        gnosemic syllable,   unspoken sound,
uttered by grass and leaf.

declaration of unfurling ferns
      bud
      new born wheat
      emerald olive jade   proclamation of

       nonfinal climaxing.

gyroscopic force holds emerging totality's configuration patterns
asserting nothing
            revealingly opulent.

      s
     p
      r
      i
       n
        g undressing chaste winter

with compelling clarity.

19.

How sad that Mr. Me and Mrs. My should whine and cry
in seeming tightness which does belie
the fretful false misshapen lie of space become a tomb.

How sad that every where becomes the why
and every now becomes the when of
sad mediocrity's bastion of because.

How sad that each and every point-less point of space
becomes the size of Mr. Me and Mrs. My and each and every
moment
of momentless time becomes a question mark in which we die.

How sad that each seeming person (an actually unseeming
divulgence of divinity's mirth) must, by dictates of dictatorial ego's
impenetrable logic, become the whine and cry of Mr. Me and
Mrs. My.

How happy to sing upon a lark of light and swoon within the
soft moonlight. To unbecome reason's endless fight and shine
and joy in great delight. Goodbye Mr. Me and Mrs. My, and now
the single seeing.

20.

It is not possible to step onto the third floor roof from the ground, a ladder is needed, a stairway. What is it that "becomes enlightened"? The unborn wisdom awareness has never changed, the body is temporary, the "self" arises in and as confusion about the authentic nature of appearance. What becomes enlightened?

My father had a friend who had a nervous breakdown due to shell shock in World War II. To compensate for the mind-shattering fear of having seen his friends blown to bits he disappeared into the delusion that he was Napoleon. He poured over maps and planned conquests. If he was confronted by the truth of his identity he went into an almost catatonic freeze. To help him the psychiatrists would bring small bits of his past into the room, a picture of his kids or wife, an object from home. They would leave these in the room, not confronting him with them, and allow him to discover them for himself. In this way, little by little, he came back to his real identity.

The spiritual path is much like this method except that forgetfulness has been so long that certain muscles of knowing ourselves, in truth, have become atrophied. The path simultaneously strengthens the weakened muscles and introduces progressive elements of our real truth into consciousness. The ability, dexterity and strength of consciousness grows. Its ability to investigate the subtle aspects of itself are fortified. In nature it is not uncommon for a series of quantitative changes to lead to a qualitative leap. When water is heated it becomes hotter degree by degree and then, suddenly, at the boiling point it makes the qualitative leap to vapor. When consciousness is made progressively subtle it eventually makes a qualitative leap and dissolves into wisdom awareness that knows its unborn and undying bliss.

Wisdom awareness is like clear light, unperceivable. This awareness needs appearances, the playful potency of its own energy, to know itself in-through-as. In this knowing there is the possibility, the likelihood, that the wisdom awareness will mistake its knowing for a "subjective entity," a self. And also mistake its luminous glow for appearances—objects. This is much the same as my father's friend mistook himself for Napoleon. This mistaken idea is not simply in the mind for, in truth, there is no distinction between mind and body. This mistake is embodied and enworlded in us and our lives. The path does not create the truth; it removes the obstacles that prevent wisdom awareness from knowing itself in and as appearances.

What becomes enlightened is the whole body. First the knowingness awakens to its deepest reality, unconfused by body and world, and then body and world are progressively drawn in, transformed, translated into beauty, truth and goodness which are the natural result of great freedom and awareness' natural affection.

21.

Kabir says: Heart herat he sakhi, raha Kabir—I was searching, searching . . . a miracle happened, the searcher disappeared. When there was no seeker, no searcher, that is the moment I found.

I fall from Heart   to sky

Along a crystal pathway   and

de

  scen

     ding

           once again (but now as only

mystery)   swim the grace full circle of

the body.

(Appearance does not imply a birth but only an appearing. As form does not imply an "other" but only brightness perceived by knowing—a symbol signaling the perfect union . . . . And Love gives birth to every one.)

Light unborn shatters across the sky of mind, and everything, and every thing, appears. The reflection of reflections, a jeweled net, a moment's pause
the extent of
adoration's
pure
intention.

Within your body   a path   a river flowing to the
sky, a temple, un

                 built   by human hands.

In that temple I fall from Heart to sky.

22.

Standing by the side of the road watching the empty field, 3:45 AM. How stainless the night sky in its union of blackness and shimmering stars. Sky/star/earth/corn/ road/hand/eye/breeze ... this appearance mystery beyond deep or shallow.

The empty net of perception, cast out, catches subtle sparkles of silver from the glint of moonlight on cornstalks and there is not even the faintest hint of "one" who perceives.

It is a joy to walk in the early morning, before the mass of people have woken from sleep and filled the world with business. Humanity is absorbed in building a fragile architecture of concept and concern. The buttresses of noise and bustle of activity hold back the awe-inspiring infinity of otherness. The thick walls of worry and apprehension form philosophical patterns of intellectualism, becoming habits of mind, body, feeling and consume the true nature and possibility of human growth.

Mind needs silence, openness, the non-humanocentric force of nature. Human beings need the immensity of nature and heart's deep silent places. Humanity needs these as they dwarf the human form and restore wonder. Most fear this and so cling to the small alcoves of self that have been carved from the known. Most people never wander the fields and streets at 3:00 AM when human concept does not rule.

The ancient Upanishadic sages called this time Brahma-mhurta, the hour of Brahma. It is translucent, resonating with blessedness and otherness. Meditation practice, the disciplines of the path, is not meant to "achieve" or "accomplish" but simply fine-tune the instrument of body, mind and feeling until it resonates with such subtle harmony that it can sink its roots in that mystery prior to knowledge.

Tassels fallen from a corn stalk make a small refuge and a rustling sound draws the body's attention. Standing perfectly still, a tiny field mouse is seen as it rushes out to pick up forgotten kernels and scurry them back to its makeshift home. The field of perception is a meaning saturated intangibility. Perception is the most intimate of acts wherein the love-making of awareness and appearance sighs with gentle caress. In this simplicity there is neither self nor other. And, even though the luminous field of perception has risen from the absolute mystery of emptiness, nothing has left anything and there is only stainless simplicity.

23.

Veneration, exaltation, elevation, deification . . . we no longer have gods to worship and what we have been given to replace them is . . . . . . opinion. Comment this, comment that, like, dislike, quick! Blurt it out with all the finesse of a bulimic's vomit filling the toilet.

Mass market, mass media, mass cultural bulimia. Commercial society has discovered that nothing sells quite so well as narcissism and so the nightly news asks you to "send in your opinion." (They care, really they do! Lol . . . no, really).

The pretense that people value your opinion, or that they should, is the opiate of the masses. Question the entrenchment of dull narcissism through the glorification of unthinking opinion! Refuse to be the slave of mass marketing disguised as social networking.

Question the authority of your opinions. Question those who would inspire you not to. Question the technology that enshrines your opinions like little golden calves, false idols of mediocrity.

Social media is to authentic dialogue what internet porn is to love. Fakebook and Liespace, the diarrhea of unexamined life, consume the potential of human birth with the mass barrage drivel.

24.

When the wind is not blowing there is no wind. When the mind is not thinking there is no mind. When there is no mind, identity (that paltry need for separation to find security) is displaced by Love.

"I think therefore I am." Descartes' famous phrase won't do for the deep philosophy of the yogi. What am I when I do not think? Am I? And, if not, then what? What of the body when there is no thought? What of perception? What is "I Am" when it is not buttressed with language, concept?

Normally, when one is not thinking, one falls into the ignorance of sleep but this is not the only option, even in sleep. The training of inner yoga offers other options. Each of the four main states of a human being 1. Waking 2. Dreaming 3. Deep sleep 4. Sex and desiring is characterized by a certain way in which consciousness becomes the enworlding of confusion. In deep sleep it is possible to draw in the luminous clarity of awareness and then a great mystery is revealed. Awareness is 24/7. Consciousness comes and goes but awareness is always. And, insofar as there is any identity to "self," it is luminous awareness not consciousness.

When each of the four states is purified of the confusions that bind it to delusion, it naturally becomes a dimension of reality. Deep sleep becomes the essence of wisdom mystery—an expanse of openness beyond even the notions *being* or *non-being*. Dream becomes the luminous dimension of bliss. The so-called waking state becomes the playful expression of bliss and emptiness. Desire becomes the ease of perception as pure pleasure, a perfect, non-frustrating act of Love. All of these are realized by the methods of tantric Buddhism.

When the mind goes where no mind goes, into alert wakefulness free from conditioning thoughts, then the mind becomes nothing more than a luminous empty spaciousness. This space is without birth or death, coming or going, suffering or the extinction of suffering. It is not advanced nor is it a beginner. It is without the fretful hierarchies of ego's suffering effort. It is not lost nor is it found. It is not asleep nor is it awake. It is not Buddhist nor Christian, nor black nor white. It is not liberated nor is it in bondage. Within this unconditioned mind there are no "things" nor is there the absence of appearances. There neither *is*, nor is there no *is*. It is not religious nor is it profane but perfectly sacred.

The essence of mind is a purity. The mind's nature is a luminous clarity that does not pervade the expanse but *is* the expanse's dimensionality. Mind's energy is the child of illusion born from the union of these two—the expanse of appearance.

25.

Yesterday someone wrote, "Can you show me God?" Yes, surely. If you come with great sincere longing thirst then, without doubt, I can show you Truth, God. The question is "Are you ready to see?" What if seeing means you must relinquish all your illusion? Nothing is kept hidden, nothing is withheld, but the lukewarm heart does not have the discipline of body and mind needed to hold such perception. Because of this, Buddha Nature remains self-secret. There is no fee other than earnestness. I can directly show you but can you see?

Have you watched the edges of the ice dance and sparkle where freeze and melt meet in flow? My hand on my beloved's, where does one warmth end, another begin? One who has gone to wisdom bliss dissolves into the lives of their friends . . . no Buddha, no sentient being, no liberation, no bondage. This silent joy is the communication beyond words and dogmas.

This urge "to be" arises from the illusion that there is Being and Non-being but, in perfect freedom of the absolute, both these are as irrelevant as a flashlight being on or off in the noonday sunlight. One who realizes Truth is free from "being" and "non-being," free from want and need—such a state is not status, it is Love. The remaining body becomes the servant of all appearance. This remainder, this body, acts as communication. It is always speaking the secret hidden name of God. It is always divulging the hidden most corner of divine nothingness' non-dimensionality.

Yes, even though there is no "I", no "showing," no "you." Yes, certainly.

26.

Just as the bright and clear heart of the sun
cannot be obscured by the darkness of a thousand eons,
The luminous heart of your own mind
Cannot be obscured by this cyclic existence of infinite eons.
—Mahasiddha Tilopa

An udumbara flower blossoms in the night.
Its scent perfumes the air. Buddhas and yogis rejoice.
Common people don't notice.

A fortunate bee gathers nectar from an opening flower,
a dung beetle nestles in dung. A tree grows with roots in
the sky and flowers in the earth of the body. Who will
notice?

Look, quick! There is something all your intellectual
knowledge can't ever grasp. It's not inside, it's not
outside.   Quick   where will you look?

Happy in my own little boat, room enough for all beings,
the stars, the whole night sky! From the muck of
confusions, a lotus blossoms, Buddhas are everywhere
and under the 4 AM milky way sky, my head becomes
full of non sense.

Different aspects—same thing Same thing—different
aspects Not two, not One, not none . . . All that is just so
many words and outside, cherry blossoms in the
moonlight.

27.

The trunk of the giant oak was thick with life and more than a century of growth. Only a few of these old giants remained along the edge of the road; the rest had been cut down to make room for humankind's activity. The massive branches formed patterns in the crisp autumn sky. The eye, drawn into that blue, finds beauty in the alternation of dark branches and open expanse—form and emptiness.

Without any thought the body walked over to the enormous trunk and placed its hands on the rough bark. The pulse of perception slowed to the rhythm of ancientness. Stillness spread across mind and feeling. In communion one was free from past, future and even the "now." Stepping back from the tree the wetness of tears felt cold in the fall wind.

We are poorer due to the loss of so many of these great old trees. Once the fields here were forests filled with trees, older by far than this oak, whose stillness filled the air with rich depth. Now the area, stripped of almost all old growth, is haunted by the uncertainty of life. It is possible to live in this world with gentleness. Now the only standing forests are filled with thin, anorexic trees. It is as if whole forests have been convinced by destructive images of fashion models in magazines.

Human life is brief and thirsts for the sense of ancientness embodied in forms of primeval life but we are destroying these and leaving our own bodies and hearts bereft. The old trees, untouched forests, wild places, all of these impart a stillness to mind and body. It is vital to feel the terrible loss of nature without the slightest effort to avoid. Let its fact wash over, and in, and through you. Its pain makes the mind strong and supple enough to question.

There can be no knowledge of oneself except in relationship—in relation to all of life. Why? Because, in truth, there is but a single body—the body of life. The enlightened wisdom that all beings seek is found in perfect relationship so intimate that there is no separation between known, knower and the knowing. In this knowledge we are the oak, and the one who cuts down the oak, and the bird who lives in the oak and the watcher of the oak.

Technology, information, knowledge, these all tend to give "mastery over" but not the wisdom of what to do with that mastery. If this partial knowing is developed lopsidedly, as within our culture, then there is deep alienation with ourselves, our bodies, nature. This alienation breeds an aggression whose hostility lashes out at the body of life. As the anorexic is at war with their embodiment, humanity is now at war with its enworldment.

The frenetic pace of technology allows for greater communication but less and less communion. Social media allows for huge amounts of talking but there is little true listening. To understand life in its wholeness, to understand yourself, or any "other," you must develop a tremendous stillness, capacity for listening, observation. For this you must face the addiction to stimulation that our culture offers to replace the loss of intimacy.

The spiritual path is a radical de-conditioning. It is to voluntarily submit to be deprogrammed from the brainwashing of the cult of modern culture. I am not saying there was some golden age in the past, or will be in the future; that is simply another fantasy replacing the need for work in this moment. What I am saying is that the work of facing the light and shadow of our personal life, our cultural conditioning and the conditioning of even the human karmas can be enacted any time anywhere and anywhen. To hold the joys and sorrows of the world without turning from one or denying the other is the key to opening the door. To face the contradictions of persona, culture, human life, without any running away opens the door to a radical transmutation of consciousness. In this transmutation the very cells of the brain are changed, as if a great natural wildfire burned away the tangled undergrowth of mind's fictions and, in the ash covered soil, the first shoots of sacredness can grow.

To know the world with open-hearted tenderness insures that one will indeed be broken hearted but also that one will know joy— both the joy of this world and an unborn joy beyond the touch of decay or corruption. In this joy one discovers a love of life, a love in life, a love that pervades life. This Love of Life knows that there must be great trees, there must be fields and wild areas unspoiled by the touch of civilization's mechanics. This Love of Life knows there must be relationship unspoiled by the wounds of memory. And, knowing this, it polishes the bright virtue of mind, moment after moment. This Love of Life grows deep roots into the soil and its branches weave tangling patterns across the sky of living.

Further down the road another great oak is marked with a red X, waiting to be cut down. Its branches had the temerity, the gall, to grow too close to the telephone lines. This offense can only be punishable by death. To interfere with the constant chatter of superficiality is a grave offense in our culture. Telephone poles, like an infinity of crosses, traverse the country so that we can chatter away while Jesus dies. Mastery over nature, pursued without wisdom, is forging alienation into the very soil, plant life, forest, wildlife and hearts of every person. The mind, still, silent, without avoidance is swept through by the wildfire of Love and grief.

28.

Midnight: I would like to live as invitation   a
mother's footsteps   weary.
                    a door with broken hinges,
                    unable to shut   authentic
                    solace   torn paper mind.

i would like to live, heart trained, breath disciplined,
each cell forged to love. each cell compassion's sleeper
cell. i would like to live the broken heart of Jesus'
mother at the foot of the cross and never turn away.

3 AM: (*look at this. the whole moon in a
dew drop. and, what's this?   it's not even
wet!*) I would like to live the body of the
dew drop, of the full moon, of the bucket
of water
                         reflections   mind's
                         patterns   open space.

    bobcat crossing field, black bear sleeps near Chen's
    hut, Khandro dreams above the shrine room like a
    swallow in its nest   patterning the   currents
    and eddies of love.

Dawn: I think of Basui, that wondrous ancient man, rice
paper skin,   master of old. First birds awaken

                    What is this
                    mind?

29.

I shone in this small shape as one who proceeds from the Father. I bubbled up and flowed out from that. I was the first emanation. I was his entire likeness and image.

—Gnostic tradition, First Book of Leu

The Long Now:

Daytime. My hair drips sweat. Your pearl teeth, in the oyster of your mouth, gleam with smiling. My skin knows touch and warmth. Your hand knows strength of purpose . . . In this Long Now between emerging and dissolving . . . water rises as wave. Falls. Rises.   Again. Same water, same tidal motion, same ocean.   Same wave?

Evening. Dim starlight emerges, come morning it resolves again into bright. A western star in twilight's land of meeting and parting . . . hands rough with earth, scars of honest work, lines etched on the face by love—some from pleasure, some from pain. These are the retirement plan of happiness.

Nightime. I lay down my head, feet, hands, shoulders, the small cares, plans, sad turns, sweet moments that mark the contours of Love's body. I lay down the slow pulse of marrow and the rhythm of blood, spinal fluid, cells. I lay down mind in the bed of ease. I lay down tomorrow and wake up in tomorrow when the play of tides again draws the deep of mind's luminosity into the frolic of appearance.

Dawn. First emanation, deep a bright arises, emerges,
resolves again in sleep, emerges once more . . . entire
likeness of bird song, the smell of grass, eyes   open
and "sight" becomes appearance

                                . . . and I will love
                          you   again, like
                          yesterday   again,   like
                          tomorrow   again,   in this
                          Long Now   again,
                          this emerging
                          again, and resolving   again

no one who has tasted the salty water can any longer
say "this wave, that one."

30.

Spiritual life is conscious evolution. From now we must participate in the unfoldment of what and who we are. Up until now evolution has proceeded without us, through us, as us. It has produced this half finished product called man, woman, humanity. But each person, somewhere deep in the chest, behind the breastbone, down in the cavern of the marrow knows—knows the work is unfinished.

There are organs of knowledge undreamt of by the mind. Ways of knowing unsuspected by the calculating machine of thought. The body is an alchemical chamber. There is mind and feeling, mercury and cinnabar; there is a fetus waiting for nourishment. When the lead of what we are goes into that cauldron what comes out is gold—the whole body as an act of knowing, immediate, direct, mysterious.

The brain with its inductive logic draws generalized conclusions from finite collections of specific data. Often wrong. It mixes, mingles, mangles bodily and emotive input with logic and spews forth superstitions such as "self," "birth," "death." In our time and culture, body and feeling go almost unrecognized and so their potentialities remain uneducated.

What we have now is useful . . . for getting to the grocery store, for the meat on meat act of reproduction, for remembering hurt and tasting the bitter flavor of resentment. It is even enough to glimpse into the shadows of another way. Shadows reflected on the wall of Plato's cave. Longing, intuition, a direction into mystery moves us to paint bison, hand prints, strange figures in red and black. We are the seed in springtime longing into a mystery that we fear and also need.

We need to know. Not as a bit of knowledge, a concept, a false idol of imagination and hope. We need to become gnostic knowing embodied, enfleshed, incarnated. Skin, brain, heart, feeling, thought all of these become something different, in the same in the way the butterfly and the caterpillar are different. But it will not happen by closing yourself up in a cocoon, waiting for nature to take its course. Nature's course for you ends in a box, six feet under. We must participate in the unfoldment of what and who we are in conscious fashion. Spiritual life is conscious evolution.

From the alchemical cocoon of "the work" emerges enworlded realization of Buddha Nature, that bright of natural awareness flowing in-through-as the structures and forms of subtle knowing. Enlightenment is as much in your toes as in your mind. If it is not then what has been realized is only a façade, a conceptual band aid.

The alchemical chamber of spiritual life gives birth to a mind that has become rooted in deep silence, an organ of feeling that dwells in and as love and a body that lives the subtle currents of joy into all appearance.

31.

Without thoughts there is no person. Who wants
to go there and see what there is?

~

My biggest secret regarding appearance: whatever
Appears—there, not there—there is a way to love
it . . . so I do!

~

Mind is full of habit. Negative habits consume
energy. Tremendous energy is needed to break the
shackles of deluded perception. Positive habits
produce energy. Change negative habits into
positive habits to go beyond all habits
(any other way is the fantasy and arrogance of immaturity).

~

To live in a climate of affection is a choice, an
action. Ego is an action. The action of withdrawal.
Tender-hearted affection is an action. The action of
love. Action requires muscles and muscles grow
strong with use.

32.

This morning the sun's rays broke the horizon, played through tree branches, shattered across ice melt in ten thousand droplets of light. Dawn slipped into daytime. Stopping to look carefully at the ice melt there was an ever shifting complexity of patterns. There is a twilight edge where ice melt meets water—neither this nor that, a state of transformation. Tiny swirling galaxies, eddies of flow and patterns of freeze played across the stones of the pathway. Body and mind went journeying into the living symbol of appearance.

Ego is always preoccupied—pre (before) and occupied. The dictionary gives the 4th and 5th definitions of occupied as "*4. To seize possession of and maintain control over by or as if by conquest. 5. To engage or employ the attention or concentration of.*" Ego is pre-occupied, occupied by its ceaseless rounds of identification, concepts, always separate from what is merely perceived. The mere appearance, which communicates a mysterious unity of emptiness and clarity, is missed. Instead mind's designated object is seen. Mind's consideration mediates between appearance and being and so a sense of alienation pervades. The problem lies in the immaturity of the adult mental mechanism. Its evolution has ceased but is not finished.

Preoccupation is immaturity. Perhaps it is better to say that ego is not so much pre-occupied as that ego *is* the preoccupation of attention. Functionality of mind is not the problem but the co-opting of all perception by this function produces a twisting and distortion of both perception and body mind. The collected stories of alienation, with its inherent discomfort, is what is experienced by mind, feeling, body as "*one's self.*" In this way "self" becomes a feedback loop of the past mediating the present moment of perceiving. Undoing, unmaking, unknowing this habit, and its effects in body, feeling and mind, is the import of our work.

A squirrel peeked out from behind a log and considered the snow and ice. Its fur was golden with sunlight. Both of us remained perfectly still and a tangible reverence filled the space between us. The awakened state is not a sentimentilization of nature but the holding of nature within the dimension of the divine. Eye, ear, touch unburdened from delusion is a most mysterious action of beauty and truth.

Walking back from my office to the house light rays still played across ice. The squirrel dipped his foot into the cold water and licked off droplets. Mind free and easy flowed with sunlight on an excursion of delight in a thousand thousand flavors . . .

33.

Meditation in solitary places make the yogi happy.
Prayers and offerings make the protectors happy.
Cash up front makes most gurus happy.
Wandering without care in the vast expanse is my happiness.

Right motivation and pure heart makes the Buddhas happy.
Fearless Conduct makes the siddha happy.
Approving glances and compliments make most disciples happy.
Wandering without care in the vast expanse is my happiness.

Teachings and instruction makes the guru's student happy.
The breadth of space makes the Garuda happy.
The tangles of mind keep most people unhappily occupied.
Wandering without care in the vast expanse is my happiness.

The beauties of puja make the devotee happy.
Blazing and dripping in secret channels makes the yogi happy.
A little wet friction makes most men happy.
Wandering without care in the vast expanse is my happiness.

Pure dharma lineage makes the practitioner happy.
The heritage of secret conduct makes the yogin happy.
Eagerly waiting inheritance makes most people happy.
Wandering without care in the vast expanse is my happiness.

Accumulating mantra makes the mantrica happy.
Counting breaths makes the zen person happy.
Tallying money makes the monastic treasurer happy.
Wandering without care in the vast expanse is my happiness.

Hearing praise of the guru makes the disciple happy.
Listening to the sound of emptiness makes the yogin happy.

Celebrity gossip makes TV watchers happy.
Wandering without care in the vast expanse is my happiness.

With the empty sky as my home,
And a happy mind as my dogma,
Like a lion who roams free
I wander the vast expanse.

A spontaneous song offered to beloved Dakinis on the
25th day of the Flower Moon.

34.

They had come from several countries to the small Paris apartment in order to listen to teachings. In the stillness of mind there is no notion "speaker" "listener" and so there is space for something subtler than communication. Communion is encounter without separation.

For decades single pointed earnestness has forged this body mind into a vehicle for joy and the sharing of joy. This accumulation is not some schlock for sale to whoever wanders in. Those who gather have varying motivations—some have merit, others most definitely do not.

The Guru is that one who has not only discovered the Unborn but become its action of Unbirthing. Guru is function not status. Within truth there is no such thing as status. The Guru is intentionless, a pure response only . . . a mirror of what you bring to the table.

The teacher of wisdom must abide in and as wisdom. Within wisdom there is no need, and appearances are known in kindhearted fondness. It is from this freedom of affection that the response to suffering, known as the teaching, arises. Radical freedom tinged by the color of love. The urge to share one's state is the only rule that crosses all boundaries of ordinary beings and Buddhas. The urge to share this pure mystery of freedom and affection molds words from emptiness, types, speaks, sings.

The Guru's body mind is the stem cell of life's total body. They manifest awareness energy as needed given context and content. The Guru's body is a remainder, left behind when the mind has gone to bliss and, now animated by the affections of infinite feelings, dances across sunlight and water, earth and feeling.

People sit silently waiting, but the waiting must be more than passive for there to be responsiveness. This body responds in the presence of true longing. Neither this body, nor the seeker, can have any idea what will happen. The unfoldment of mystery is the joy of spiritual life. Sometimes the play of seeker and Guru is a symphony of beauty; other times it is a thud of tedious uselessness. It all depends on what is brought by the one who wishes response.

35.

A little song by a drunken tantrica

Two great millstones, devotion and practice,
grind the grain of mind's concepts.
The pot of the body, heated by the bliss of inner fire,
boils the water of life.

The sugar of the Guru's word,
catalyzes the yeast of mind's functioning,
dying in wisdom it becomes the deathless liquor.
Where is the yogi who can brew this strong beverage?

Anger, pride, lust, envy, ignorance—
these five poisons become the nectar of gods.
Gulped down the throat of intense preparation,
intoxication in wisdom is the bliss of unborn freedom.

The hum of mantra resonates in the drunken Heart,
this song is sung to the tune of unknowing.
Let others accumulate their knowledge from books,
Traktung drinks the blood of delusion and is freed.

36.

Solar Dynasty: a country for appearance

intensity extensity   sky and expanse

          mind settles

               into its ownmostness.

luminosity is information   concept, disinformation.
pathways imply direction   but location has no
place in space
direction implies destination   but there are no such
agendas

communication without implication

        tree sky table earth sofa fruit   curve of arm
and cheek   the simple memory   eye, face, touch,
tender

               line

               drawn

               from   form less ness to
mind's trans   lucence   ing.

Communication implies an "other," but implication is
only rumor. The touch, line of feeling, tender love drawn
from eye to form, feeling, into births, myths of name and
form, magnolia blossoms and the warmth of summer
nights . . . all these are, and are not, and both and neither.

Some mystery becomes   display of pre-ontological
symbols, wonder's patterning.   Mind becomes
dimensionality   tree sofa earth wife fruit table father.

Dimensionality implies direction → direction implies agenda
→ implies evolution → but this simple presence-ing is not
so complex.   Mind,   complexity in simplicity,

a country for

appearance.

Afterthought: A country for appearance.

*The manner in which the ceaselessly open vastness of pure mystery becomes a dimensionality, in which appearance rises and falls as the dynamic of mystery "itself," is exactly what is "known" by the sage.

By "known" is meant lived . . . by "lived" is meant something more mysterious than birth and death . . . and what is *not* meant is bit or piece of intellectual knowledge. One can "be" this mystery but never know it as proposition or concept (and even "be" is impossible since it is beyond "being" or "non-being" . . . out here (which is no-where) language falls apart without its glue of "to be" of "is" and "is not."

To know in "the biblical sense".

*Luminosity pervades the expanse . . . the expanse is created by the pervasion . . . concept is perversion of pervasion but luminosity is knowing without concept— a luminous ignorance.

Pure information is living droplets of gnosis brilliant bright form and emptiness. Knowing of appearance— identity of emptiness.

*Mystery becomes dimensionality and pervasion becomes appearance and yet nothing has left anywhere and no "thing" has been born of in any "place" . . . such mysterious use of language describes the boundaries of this country for appearance.

37.

The mind, sensitive and alert yet unmoving, embraces
appearance with a tender-heartedness beyond
imagination. Senses and sense fields meet in
tremendous delicacy, their union the act of lovers. The
aggregates and elements that make up this world are
discovered to be symbols divulging divinity.
AwarenessAppearance becomes a single word.

∽

A mystery, an expanse of purity and luminosity, puts on
a clown mask called "Being." I parades and trumpets "I
Am." Being's chubby thighs chafe. Being dresses up in
drag and plays to San Fran happy crowds. Being puts on
goatee beard and speaks in Brad Pitt's voice. Being says,
"Look! Don't you think my Hello Kitty outfit is
attractive?!" Being wears scary mask of birth and death.
Being leaves no forwarding address. Being is the
expanse of truth's standup comedy routine. Sometimes
the crowd doesn't laugh.

∽

Even if you give space a name it feels no identity and so
unborn wisdom mind says, "I am nothing." The radiance
of wisdom, the dynamic of Love says, "I am every
'thing'." The five-element body play is the living
emblem, of this paradox—this complementarity.
To abide here, with no "one" who abides and no "place"

where abiding happens is the freedom place of the fully enlightened state.

*In the kitchen 4 AM, the cup fell from hand to floor, shattered. Mind like sunlight scattered   across this and that and you ask   "But where does it come from?"   and I answer "From nowhere at all sweetheart. No where at all."
Oh my love, how I long to share with you this torn paper mind,   glued edges of word, syntax, concept
                    —words like "birth"
                              "event"
                              "appearance"
                              "other"   like the
strong hands of my father folding

nothingness   into origami
shapes . . . birds, a swan, a tiger.

Love settles like twilight into the dark nighttime myth of "here," it becomes the dream of "now," but nowhen and nowhere could hold the gentleness of only this.

38.

Do not think that discarding the biotic force [means that you become]
your very self [on the contrary it is death].
> —Advayavajra, Herbert Guenther. Note 58, Notes to
> Doha Translations.

Some Notes on Urban Agriculture:

and you smelling of strawberries,
of grass,
dirt,
damp of forest floors.

a vertical landscape,
urban garden,
architecture of love's unfoldment
                    greening across hip, curve, thigh . . .

lower, a sweet

moss

scent.

sweet brown Harlem girl, blood orange,
juice spilled
all
at
once   welcome home Lucinda.

39.

A dakini night poem: A wounded heart in the month of miracles: (recollecting a conversation with Guru Pema on how we appear again and again)

He said: "You will remember, like a quick wisp, a small flutter . . . there then gone.

You will remember the prowling of streets and the way your fingers brushed across the twilight. You will remember the buzzing of little bees and the extent of silence, you will remember conflict and loss, thickets of berries, the hands of a small child, the spokes of a wheel, the fragrance of night air, the tangle of your consort's hair, conversations of sunlight.

You will remember all this and your heart will break into a thousand shard like wounds and each of these will become a form, a body, a water moon, a magical appearance, a rainbow, a mirage, a dream, a moment's hope."

I replied: "There is no rainbow, no mirage, no water moon. There is no one to see it and nothing to be seen. This virtuous moment has never been and will never end. No Buddha descended, no beings were lost, no dream like victor saved them from diseases they never had. No suffering, no end of suffering and so on right up until . . . this moment."

He said: "Yes, and still your heart will break, and still the bitter sweet pain will fill you, and still the myriad worlds will turn and spin, and still you will appear again and again until every being who never was is freed from suffering."

I replied: "This is a hard bargain you drive."
He said: "Yes, but it's the only game in town."

Night was falling into silence. The twilight sun splayed in a thousand rays and droplets. Mind from the heart flowed through the corridor of the eyes and became the only love. It is not that I was wrong, rather, it was simply that he was right. The fragrant flower closed in upon itself as dusk turned to dark.

40.

It is like an eye that sees and yet guides nothing in seeing that it may see, for the seeing is without being.
> —the 18th-century mystic, Jacob Böhme

In this dark moonless night I will lay down and let mind go where no mind goes, to brightness in expanse of truth—most people call it sleep but in spiritual awakening it is quite the opposite. But then what most call "the waking state" is truly only sleep.

When mind's functions and knowledge have gone to slumber in the deep of sleep, there is seeing without being—lucky is the one who wakes up without leaving this state of perfect unknowing all knowingness.

When concept has laid itself down to rest and there is only silence in the deep of sleep then "self" is gone. "Self" was only ever a pesky concept, a little misunderstanding between knowing and sunlight. "Self" was just an argument with "other"—shadow boxing with emptiness. When self has finally gone to sleep, forever, then knowledge gives way to knowing. Body functions without presumptions of birthing, death or other. Feeling is knowing, expansive across appearance as love.

The waking state with its confusion of self and other is, in fact, a deep sleep within ignorance. Knowing and seeing without being is, in fact, a perfect wakefulness. It knows both the iceberg's tip, called appearance, and also the expanse of unborn wisdom affection, which supports it.

In the deep of sleep there is awareness in the midst of unconsciousness. Awareness is always. To understand the difference between awareness and consciousness—which is the functioning of awareness through the senses *plus* the dysfunctionality of "self"—is the first step of wisdom. Awareness is mystery without even the notion "being." It is seeing without being. Seeing as freedom.

41.

The deep snow is beginning to melt and forms rivulets of water that carve the creek bed deeper and deeper. Walking in the woods this morning the smell of old leaves and wet earth offer a deep joy, a hint of spring. Over by a dead and rotted tree stump the green of moss announces the possibility of color in the midst of Michigan's winter grey.

Sitting at the table: "What do you see?" she asks. I see all appearances, the beauty of wonderment expressed in purity. I see the realm of confusion that beings live in; but I see it as shifting currents of compassion called beings. I see appearance seeking optimal expression in the midst of constricting delusion and then this body, mind, feeling responds spontaneously as activity to speed optimization—a self correcting mechanism of tender heartedness.

Can human beings let go the past, allow the leaves of last season to fall and rot and

be forgotten as compost for the new? When mind is filled with the old, with resentments, judgments of others actions, pains and pleasures, there can be no room for the subtle beauty emerging within each moment. If we ceaselessly mold the stream of memory into a river of opinion, our lives will run toward the ocean of stagnation. Mind must be made fresh in meditation, allowed to go where no mind goes, into the ocean of Silence and Stillness.

It is most definitely possible that there is a way and path, many in fact. What is deep and true in life is unconditioned, even by the path. The path is not conditioning but a process of unconditioning—reversing mind's habit of conditioning itself. It is for this reason that the path makes itself obsolete in success. The path is like a fire placed in a hollow log, it burns away the log and then disappears itself. Contrary to what some have said, the stainless, nonconditioned state of truth does not negate the need for the path when lost in confusion; normal sight is restored by removing cataracts. Cataract surgery does not contradict the effortless quality of normal sight. It simply removes the obstacle to it.

To die in each moment is to allow the past to become the rich soil for the new. It is in allowing the past to be past that a tremendous sensitivity arises in the mind. . . a sensitivity beyond the structures of politics and tradition. For this the muscles associated with perception and attention must have been tuned with great care.

A branch has fallen across the creek and the snow melt has found a new pattern. Washing away dirt, a beautiful red stone has been revealed. Its rough contour is colored with a streak of black and a vein of quartz. Formed by the unimaginable pressures of glacial action it has remained hidden for ten thousand years. A mind made sensitive through meditation washes away the soil of opinion and prejudice revealing hidden beauty.

42.

Wanting nothing, having nothing, being nothing this is the freedom of the sage.

Here the spontaneous luminosity shines and shimmers as all experience, perception. Appearing but never actually implying anyone or anything. Appearance does not imply birth, it only signals appearing. The unborn wisdom awareness does not deny appearance, only birth.

Within a dream there is no birth and yet there are appearances. There is the appearance of space and time and characters within the dream and yet there is no "space" inside the head through which actually existent dream entities are walking. Just so this "waking state" appearance.

There is appearance and knowing, that is all. This does not imply actual substance or being—reality, the truth, is far more mysterious than that. In truth there is no identity at all and yet there is knowing and appearing. The sage remains in the disposition of no identity in the midst of appearing and so is not convicted of the crime of birth and death.

Body has its wants, needs, propositions in relation to the dream play of seeming being, but the sage does not take their stand *as* those. All appearing, with its implied and stated demands is nothing more than a temporary shifting play, modification of light and knowing. Taking one's stand in the Nothingness state, all this shifting and shattering of light as color and form is no more, or less, than the potency of pure awareness in its appearing state.

If the whole universe were to disappear this instant it would not change the disposition or reality of the sage in the slightest;

that mystery which is knowingness would simply abide prior to being or consciousness in the knowingness of nothingness. If appearances arise again then it would abide in the knowingness of appearances.

Body looked into essence and found a place of perfect freedom bursting with syllables whose only meaning was love. Self became transparent and "that mystery" now looks through body at world, admiring the handiwork of the Beloved. Body, mystery, looks, freedom . . . all these words attempt to stretch language indicating the birthright of every being.

43.

God flows out from the Godhead as all things and yet never leaves the Godhead.

—Meister Eckhart

The cat was motionless, every muscle poised to strike and yet utterly relaxed. It waited; still, silent, alert, it waited for its prey. Nature is a play of oppositions in harmony. Can we be so still within, so patient that we are able to wait for the right action to arise? For this we have to give up fascination with every passing whim of mind or emotion. Can we sit within stillness until stillness becomes us and then, from within that and without leaving that, allow action to arise from a tremendous stillness?

Conditioned mind has no patience. Frantic, tight, it can only survive through fretful activity, occupied in every moment by distraction, fixation, identification. This state of disharmony arises from a malfunctioning of mind's activity. This malfunctioning, that has become the human norm, is a degenerative habit. Mind's natural state is one of vast openness, expansiveness and silence. Only rarely does it need to churn out concepts.

The path is designed to ease us from our addiction to malfunction's content so we might relax into the context—the spacious expanse of mind's natural ease and silence. The content of mind is the union of appearance and identification. Identification arises from the fact that awareness' clear light nature takes on the color of whatever it perceives. If you put clear glass on blue cloth what you will see is the blue. It takes great maturity for the unborn awareness to not lose cognizance of its nature in the midst of perception. Identification begins with the notion "I Am" (even god suffers that one), proceeds to I am the body, I am the mind, I am this and that.

When one cuts through identification then one slips out from the prison of content into context—the matrix of luminous awareness felt as Being, the "I Am," the first confusion. But this is not the end. Beyond this there is still a pure, irreducible mystery beyond Being and non-being to be discovered. Beingness itself dissolves into an unnamable mystery—prior to consciousness. Here there is no high or low, no bondage or enlightenment, no self or other— only mystery beyond, within and as everything and every thing. Then body lives as the act of Love and the slave of Love.

The cat, bored with his game, stood and walked away. Every muscle relaxed, free from the past.

44.

POV (point of view)

where arrogance (self-other) is left behind
         point of view collapses
         (affection overwhelms)
today tomorrow.

It used to seem more complex. But that was only because of
PointOfView, that demand to account for confusion mind
thought concept with logics of where why because and if.   But,
when perception ceases to imply location (when concept has let go
of strategy)   then   only

simplicity.

First there were sentient beings. Then there was
Buddha. Now ...... a collection of ordinary moments
...... without ...... reference   to   PointOfView. Let
me tell you about realizing Buddha:

> *A card table against the wall, legs folded in.*
> *Jesus dies on the cross (not for our sins*
> *but because of them). The tremble of leaves*
> *at twilight. A coffee table covered in symbols*
> *of the everyday. Lao Tzu turns down the*
> *emperor's offer. Mozart is born. Dogs play*
> *tug of war with a sock. The liberation of*
> *Auschwitz. Carpet cleaners lift a sofa. Sleep*
> *becomes waking. Perception is born.*

Simplicity   speaks   the language of
affection   in the angle of my wife's face, dew
soaked woodland flowers at dawn, the sound of leaves,
bills in the mail.

    Affection for appearance.
    Affection for non-appearance.
    Affection for the impossibility of self

      and
          Other.

45.

forget how to count
starting with your own age
starting with how to count backward
starting with even numbers
starting with Roman numerals.
        —W.S. Merwin, *Migration*

The Guru whispered in my ear and the structure of my life crumbled. More than this the very act of structuring was unmasked; from then on it has all been forgetting. I lost everything and every thing. And now?

This body, the "I" of life, sits here in its own little boat. Neither big nor small but just enough room for all of playful appearance to be cradled, it floats on the ocean of pure mystery. Cradled the way a loving mother cradles her child's face in her hands ….. how could I ever speak to you a word that would describe this tender-hearted affection for every appearance. Light flows out from the Heart, a song bird breaks the spell of winter.

Here in my own little boat, just the size of every thing and Nothing, no being has ever been born or died, no one has suffered and no One need be realized. And yet … and yet, love flows from heart to eye to space to beings. In truth's abode there are no "things" and still—no child left behind, no appearance uncared for. There is no "truth" outside Love.

Here in my own little boat—words left behind, concepts laid to rest in the grave of the dimensionless space of perfect reality. Mind is at ease. Carefree, bliss is everywhere as every "thing"

. . . . and "identity"? . . . identity is just the passing whim of Nothingness' play. All doubt gone in Luminous Ignorance, and light pervades the everyplace of ceaselessness.

I have lost every "thing," "name," and "form." Status and the game of hope and fear has toppled like a house of cards. This blood drinker says, "Oh yogi if you wish to know the simple path, give up pretension and clasp the Guru's feet to your heart."

In my little room called, AwarenessAppearance, there is only love. The room *is* only love. Buddhas, beings, gods and men rise and fall like waves. Like sparkling light on the dancing ocean. Sitting in my little room I write love letters to all existence, invitations, seductions. Painted with the ink of delight on the stainless paper of perception.

46.

Torn Paper Mind on a sleepless night

2AM

The body is love. The body is light made the illusion of substance. The body is the identity of all appearance. Free from all self-concern the body becomes a mystery uncontrived and free.

3AM

The body is a single and whole, the body of life. The body is never separate from heartbreak. Love knows Christ and the one who murdered Christ—inseparable.

4 AM

Silence fills the body. Mind has gone to nothing. Space extends and its extension is the unfolding of mystery. Love, wound, bliss all find their ease and rest.

6 AM

From silence comes dawn light. Worlds and beings awaken in the kangaroo pouch of Being. Filaments of light form the body. The heart of mystery puts on the shirt of appearance. Body, taken off the hanger in the closet of Nothingness, makes a fashionable statement.

47.

People had come from various places in Germany to listen to "this" talk. The flight had been long and there was a deep pressure in the head from the weariness of long travel. There is a strange beauty that overshadows the body during any teaching. During a teaching nothing negative can be felt physically. The body is protected by a subtle yet profound power. Mind and heart become flooded by unbearable tender-heartedness. Awareness reaches out as perception to touch the lives of any who come.

The hall was of the Drikung, filled with images, statues, and the paraphernalia of practice. It is all familiar to this body and there is a deep understanding of meanings. The Tibetan tradition is filled with beauty and also the possibility (often actualized) of greed, posturing, politics and the conditioning of mind and heart. Any endeavor that mixes power, wealth and spiritual hopes is open to profound corruption. It is exactly the corruption that the European traditions rejected after the dark ages of the church. Sometimes corruption is more palatable when dressed in exotic clothing.

A woman has come, desperate with great sorrow over the death of a loved one. She is here seeking solace, comfort, for that is the function of exoteric religion. But there is a deeper possibility than simply covering her grief with lullabies and mytho-poetic stories of after death. Can she be helped to remain utterly still with her feelings without any attempt to mold them to a pre set pattern. Can she hold feeling in consciousness without any attempt to escape; without even the tiniest fraction of a movement in mind. This is called Mahamudra, the great gesture of awareness, in the Drikung tradition.

When mind does not move at all there is innocence. This innocence is an active power that untangles the heart. This innocence is beyond the ego's stages of grief, all very rational, all very correct—very partial. In stillness every feeling will divulge the entire working of mind and also something sacred behind mind.

Sadly this woman does not have the strength of mind and heart necessary to perceive the constant jumping away from the "as is." The path is a series of maneuvers in consciousness that strengthen the muscles necessary for the great gesture of naked perception.

Sitting, naked in the sorrow of her sorrow, there is the paradox of the path and the unconditioned result. Out in the hall many people with their varying hopes and expectations wait for a teaching on the path.

48.

The unborn wisdom essence is without nationality, race, religion, creed. The luminous Buddha Mind transcends contrivance, concept, tradition and lineage. Their sign is not found in status or pomp—cannot be revealed or hidden. Whoever knows "this" mysterious brilliance is mysterious brilliance itself—unchanging through all changes, waking, sleeping, living or dead.

∞

Appearance is a line traced through mystery; like when you move your hand through bioluminescent algae in the ocean and leave a path of light. This line, a curve of light and sound, trace the inscrutable exquisiteness of mystery. The sigh of love when arc of hip and belly fall down thigh into calf. It traces the map of leaves forming overlapping colors in autumn, the vulnerability of steel and glass, the ambush of impermanence.

∞

This place of living is a room and the room is only love, but its truth can be unknown when the dark and restless shadow of confusion eclipses the sun of wisdom bliss. These methods, this path, this beautiful trajectory of Vajrayana is such a force that it removes the endarkened dullness restoring the vision of what has been true all along—true but unseen.

49.

spring,   then summer, and with fall impermanence
takes its fee.

       winter: white bloom on winter's dark
       branch. The   impossible   playing
       of light and shadow,

          sunlight
          and I whisper Mori's name.
She whispered in my ear "you are not what you think
yourself to be." Seed of longing broke open and the
flower of trust blossomed. Now mind, gone to nothing in
spacious ease delights, frolics, in fields of luminous play-
full-ness.

Not two, not one, a mystery beyond concept. Mori, her touch, her
lips . . . . . . and body has become the simple act of Love.

When mind holds perception in the delicacy of Silence
this is Mori's hand on my arm. Sight, feeling, thought
without any trace of aggression   harmony extends
and   Deep Silence   all life happens
for this

          unfathomable Silence   is

divine presence.

Mori whispered: The "unborn" does not deny appearance it only
denies birth. That people think they are born, that they die, is a
cause of great sadness giving rise to compassion.

And now   . . . .

50.

The stars about the beautiful moon again hide their radiant shapes,
when she is full and shines at her brightest on all the earth. —Sappho

. . . .　I'ness is the little tension,
right there at the

> heart of reason. A small confusion
> mistaking knowingness for
> subjectivity, mistaking
> luminosity's play of intangible
> appearances for "stuff."

> Apprehender Apprehended,
> misapprehended, become
> an ache like the death of
> children "before their time,"
> like　　the echo at the
> bottom of the drunk's
> bottle, like . . . . .　　like . . . . .
> suddenly, waking up to
> remember you once knew
> your wife, or, there was a
> time your children liked you.

I'ness is the financial capital behind endless projects,
monuments, attempts. It is the debit card of hopes and
fears—always endeavoring the overdraw but falling
short of the actual purchase.

I'ness is the capitol of every world, city, state, person. It
is the president of the polis of the body—a petty

dictator pretending to democracy. I'ness is where cattle cars filled with Jews on their way to *Arbeit Macht Freni* find their rationalization.

I'ness is the vehicle of birth and death's ceaselessness.

I'ness appears again and again throughout the realms of Being ..... as "Being" and "realms" are merely confusions arisen in the moment of I'ness. Where confusion does not appear then I'ness, Am'ness, Being, realms, self and other are not but the mystery of AwarenessAppearance shines beyond is and is not.

51.

In 2008 a yogini practicing at Blazing Jewel Mountain (t.k.'s solitary retreat land) asked t.k. for a small prayer for remembering the Guru so that she would never be separate from him. Laughing happily, he explained that a yogi is unlike an ordinary person because they are someone who realizes the substanceless wisdom bliss that abides as Guru and sangha within the vajra body. Through the sublime function of the body mandala and the inner yogas they go beyond meeting and parting. To recognize the true inner nature of the Guru's mind, speech, body, sangha and tsog feast one is forever delighted in remembering the Guru.

Yoginis practicing in woodland solitude,
delight in always remembering the Guru,
in order to never suffer from separation,
there are just a few little things a tantrica should recall.

Mind's own good natured formlessness,
radiant as the uninhibited jewel of activity,
concept recognized liberated on the spot,
isn't this the very mind expanse of my own precious Guru?

Sounds, uninvited, not rejected,
machinery's roar, the love trill of song birds,
unceasing shower of compassionate instruction,
isn't this the very speech of my own precious Guru?

In the emptiness expanse Original Innocence
clarity's bright virtue gives birth to magical appearance—
Remembering emptiness and clarity, not two,
isn't this the very face of my own precious Guru?

In the city of the central channel, wisdom bliss' magical
playground
aggregates elements display the deities
sense and sense fields are bodhisattvas,
isn't this the very sangha of my own precious Guru?

Indivisible mind and winds bring Chandali's exaltation,
an offering pleasing to heroes and dakinis
who abide in the city of the chakra channels.
Isn't this the very tsog gathering of my own precious Guru?

Yogini who practices purely in mountain retreat,
there is no cause for fear of separation,
a tantrica contains within their very own body
the Guru and gathering, the delight of great bliss.

5%.

Standing, dwarfed by the Eiffel Tower's mass of steel, body feels joy and beauty. People go up and down taking pleasure in the Paris views and each other's company. A girl in the elevator smiled, her mind was utterly pure, silent, and filled with beauty. There are sublime beings, hidden from almost all, in the most ordinary places. Without contrivance or even intention their liberated wisdom enacts effects on all those around them, without anyone ever knowing. Hidden sages.

No one noticed her. Peace pervaded her face and she simply stood amidst the crowd in the elevator. At the top of the tower she looked out over the city, enveloping it in her silent joy. After some time she came down the elevator again and walked away. Her body did not know the past. Her mind was free from the scars of ego. No one noticed her and yet her blessings had flowed across Paris from the Eiffel Tower's height. Watching her, body was filled with benediction, every cell.

On what does consciousness happen? Beingness, consciousness, happens somewhere, on something—like images played across a screen. Appearances happen inside of consciousness like the currents and eddies within a deep lake, but where does consciousness happen? It is impossible to know the answers to these questions in conceptual mind. You can not "know" the answer to what is prior to consciousness but you can discover you are that. The body can abide in and as that and enact its qualities in the world. The girl's mind was rooted in a deep space beyond even being and non-being. Her body was that mystery's animation.

The deepest aspect of the path is prior to consciousness. The perceiving of the world and of beingness flows out as the active potential of "that"—a pure irreducible, unutterable, mystery. It is not a new identity—it is beyond identity.

The girl, maybe 19 or 20 years old, was a treasure in the ruin of humanity's confusion and struggle. Her eyes spoke of knowing and love to anyone who knew how to look into their wonder. Even though no one seemed to notice that they were in the presence of a blessed one, still their lives would be enriched through even this minimal, unconscious, contact. Such a wonder, the hidden ones.

53.

A commentary on the names of the four huts on Blazing Jewel Mountain—the West Virginia retreat land. (Two retreat huts, Rinpoche's hut, and the kitchen hut.)

<u>Bright Virtue (hut 1)</u> is simply the self-illuminating nature of empty space. The unity the Nothingness State and the clarity of awareness is an expanse where spontaneous magical illusions cavort.

<u>Virtuous Conduct (hut 2)</u> is the natural activity of Bright Virtue. Mind, free from identification and delusions, moves in through as appearance enacting the diverse qualities of wisdom, bliss and compassion.

<u>Kunzang Dechen Ling</u> (Rinpoche's hut whose name means Gathering Place of Bliss) is the spaciousness of liberated mind cavorting with appearances. The Guru is just this—the bliss field of Bright Virtue and Virtuous Conduct.

<u>Rasa Mandir</u>—the temple of flavors—is playful appearances tasted by space's happy tongue. It is the place where beauty is formed from substance for the nourishment of all.

This is how and where we truly live.

With Being, every hand is a losing one. The odds ALWAYS favor the house. Being dresses in school girl plaid skirt to make Japanese porn. Being says LOOK it's PUSSY!!! Then everyone forgets they're going to die while Being sneaks up behind them with a big knife. (Borrowed from the set of *Psycho*). Being has no shame. Being is the best dirty joke ever told. Birth is the straight man; death is the punch line.

54.

A little ditty for my friend Arne whose summer in Germany had little sun in it—

In the mind-heart's pure devotion, Love shines as the sun of vivid happiness without cause or reason!

Within generation phase's clear appearance, all made of brightness, there is no gloom or shadow of ego's endarkening power! (even in Germany's gloom)

Within completion phase's 16 kinds of joy there is dazzling illumination, the sun of wisdom shining in the spacious expanse.

Within the deep of mind there is innate luminosity, a sphere without center or boundary—even in the midst of deep sleep!

Within the Heart of awareness there are five-colored shimmering lights ... traveling up the crystal pathway to the water lamps (eyes) their spontaneous brilliance is the cause of all appearance!

Not relying on ego's overcast sky, not wandering samsara's dark forest path, the one who has taken up the way discovers uncaused light whose brilliance becomes the display of rays and droplets.

Wishing you happiness from the misty mountains of West Virginia.

55.

What could I offer to you? The loneliness of the moon?
Deserted daytimes abandoned on city streets, 4:00 AM?

> The high tide of empty perception
> as the boat of Being alights on
> the further shore?

> The taste of cherries
> vanquishing the turmoil of
> this and that?

> Perhaps this bag of bones—
> but I did not make it, and so, is it
> really mine to offer?
> I am not even sure whose it is—
> abandoned
> as it was upon my front porch.

I would offer my mind but, having searched everywhere
for it, I cannot
find it anywhere and besides you already got the same.

Nothing, everything, something like that.
Heart filled with emptiness
I taste the void space of coming and going
here on the distant shore of 4:00 AM.

56.

Walking through the field, a stillness embraced the earth and everything was sanctified within its peace. Suddenly there was the in-rushing of wonderment. Body and breath could barely move under the weight of such immensity, such profound beauty. The body encountered a huge maple tree; its thousands of leaves rippled in the breeze forming a ceaseless alternation of colored patterns. Not wishing to disturb the sacredness permeating the environment, the body stood perfectly still.

Branches silhouetted by moonlight spread across the dark, and on the other side of the tree was a deer standing. Deer and body both still, both minds silent, life was filled with benediction. Beyond this, life was benediction.

To be in silence with old trees, whose roots sink into the earth touching water and soil, whose branches embrace the sky, changes something within the human structure. The deer also felt it. In the presence of sacredness the tree, deer and body were in harmony. Immensity, profundity came easily to the mind as meditation and the continuity of being was felt viscerally within blood, flesh and bone. Heartbeat slowed, breath became almost still, and without thought the head bowed with gratitude.

The effects of meditation can not be brought to the body by force. Its silent beauty in cell and form cannot even be invited, it is the simple disclosure of blessedness unfolding within the silent womb of an uncorrupted heart. It is our task to untangle the knots of body, mind and heart so that silence and love can come …….. sudden, uninvited. One can ready oneself; one can become a pregnant pause of longing …….. but the heart of meditation, silence, and love cannot be coerced. If we forget this then effort to attain will lead to the inevitable deceptions and illusions. When this happens, then mind becomes a fortress of insensitivity and the spiritual path ceases to be what it is meant to be.

The great maple's branches were a mantle of tranquility. There is no way to tell how long the body stood there. A dragonfly alighted on the dry grasses. The first birds of morning began to chirp. The deer, suddenly, looked to the west and ran off. Life was awakening in harmony with dawn and the first, almost imperceptible, light touched the vast extent of sky.

57.

Gentle mist covered the ground at 5 AM, a soft damp on blades
of grass soaked through my shoes and the scent of earth filled
the nostrils. Walking in the deep woods the sound of birds,
just waking, mingled with the peep of frogs. Sound met ear . . .
mystery! Awareness spread across perception and wonder welled
up in the body as if from a deep unseen spring. When the ego's
hold on the senses is relaxed then life flows through eye, ear, touch
and beauty is known.

There is no place for self-importance in truth. There cannot even
be the self-importance of a goal. Life is only direction intending
toward mystery. Direction is an ever-shifting play within the
resonances of the "as is." Simply being awareness within the "as
is" is all that is asked. In the sensitivity of this, body will respond
and, from its responses born from silence and love, there will be
direction.

The path of Tantric Buddhism teaches the mind to be still and
silent yet body to be dynamically alive and active. The eye meets
sight and, without contrivance, the dance of beauty and love is
what is known. Ear meets sound, two most intimate lovers. Touch
meets form and intimacy is born. All of these abide within the
luminous dimension of awareness flowing through body.

The realization of awareness' unborn essence is only half the
equation of realization. Realization of the manner in which
awareness flows through body and feeling as incarnation of love is
the other half.

The mountains here were ancient when the Himalayan mountains
were just born. The great scope of life fills this place. Suddenly,

out from a thorn thicket, a small rabbit came bounding in circles kicking up its feet. Laughter filled the body. Mind was as old as the mountains. Body was as young as the rabbit. Feeling was as expansive as sky.

Walking down through the woods to the Guru Rinpoche rock, body was filled again and again with the mirth that is born from ease and freedom. When mind is free there is not even the slightest iota of self importance and because of this body is free to marvel at the wonder of everything and everyone. To be no one, nothing, this is the great joy.

58.

Dzogchen Mind and a Clean Room
A Poem for my Friend Al who Never Cleans his Room

The spacious room of awareness,
free from the clutter of distraction,
is the true home to all beings.

The floor swept clean of all muddle,
is discovered to be the all basis wisdom,
the dance hall named EVAM.

The window of intrinsic knowing,
free from conceptuality's dust,
looks on empty appearance with joy.

The shirts and trousers of the five senses
neatly hung in the closet of no more clinging
are the functioning of freedom.

The bed of deep meditation, carefully made,
is the awakening place of great completion.
Oh yogi this is the joy of a clean room!

How happy when life is made simple . . .   AH!

59.

Reality is neither inaccessible, nor attainable, for it is beyond all such notions. The yogi who rests there is untouched by lust for comfort, lust for name, lust for sex, lust for power, lust for freedom, lust for enlightenment. They desire nothing and fear nothing. Die while alive and the body will become only this ease of Unborn Wisdom Love.

∾

If you watch, just watch, as mind and body fall into sleep then there are great mysteries to be discovered. Sleep is not only *not* a waste of time but is, in fact, the most active and valuable part of our day. How does mind know how to turn off senses? What is mind when dreams stop and deep sleep emerges? One must have extreme curiosity about everything. What is desire? Why? What is "seeing"? Where does mind go in sleep? Without extreme questioning then there is no purpose to life at all.

∾

I saw a bird fly through the sky—never again could mind be content with less than freedom. I heard the springtime song of frogs and crickets—heart burst into Love's longing. Reality was not hidden, love was not absent—only the mind-heart was endarkened by the cataracts of ignorance. Now lover and Beloved are one and all sight and sound have become the freedom of love.

60.

A little song about last night's delighting at the Tsog Feast Family Reunion:

My father gave me two gifts, which I treasure and keep in the amulet of my heart. First: taking no pleasure in possessions I am content in the palace of appearance. Second: having no care for status I am free from praise and all blame.

My mother drew me aside and whispered these words as inheritance: "Seeing the real as unreal there can be no chance of liberation. Seeing the unreal as real there is only entanglement and death."

My brother brewed up some strong liquor and I drank it. The home brew of great stainless intoxication opened the treasure trove of space.

My sister sewed clothing from vision, luminosity's thread sparkling golden. Mind's home is an empty house—the tsog khang. Body's abode the magical gathering palace.

Its foundation stone is made of illusion; its front door opens on space. The shrine room is luminous vision. The room of this feast is called samaya. The Vajra family gathers inside the body to eat the meal of single taste.

Enjoying this directionless assembly's enjoying is the lineage of tantricas. Without point of view, the yogin's mind is delighting, like a young stallion's frolicking joy!

61.

Dear Friend, you asked for a few simple words to remind you what it is to be a yogi. You also asked if I would write a prayer whereby you could remember me. Well, I have no interest in you remembering me . . . so, if you can use this for the same purpose then so be it.

Homage to the stainless heart of victorious ones!
Homage to invariant light!
Homage to the result, which exists as the cause!
Homage to ground Dharmakaya!

Glorious Heruka, tamer of those hard to tame, Lord of the Tantras cavorting in great bliss, the Jewel of Activity—Mind itself, the great Vajradhara, to inseparable appearance emptiness I bow down.

Magical appearance of ceaseless compassion,
Kaya of the single family of the great secret,
To the warming rays of wisdom and love,
To The Guru Pema Tro Tren Tsel, I bow down.

Father Lama, who is only kindness, special deity, who is the noble dharma, assemblage of Vajrayogini, noble sangha, to the three roots I bow down.

This body, a mandala of secrets, its heart is the Heart of all Sugatas, its pleasures are the outer offering, its kleshas are the inner offering and inseparable wisdom bliss suffices for the secret offering! To a yogi obstacles and easy times are pretty much the same.

In the playful realm of ceaseless manifestation
Here and there are an infinite palace.
Realize this and you won't need to go wandering.
To a yogi coming and going are pretty much the same.

In the dimension of luminosity and lucidity
Strangers and companions are both the deity.
Realize this and love will find its own place.
To a yogi friends and foes are pretty much the same.

In the great indestructible bindu's stronghold
Mind remains unborn no matter how many lives you've had.
Realize this and you won't fret over who you were and who
you will be. To a yogi being born or dying are—pretty much the
same.

In the vast of Mind's own way of abiding
Emptiness and appearance are mere words.
Realize this and you will be able to rest at ease.
To a yogi doing and non-doing are pretty much the same.

Listen fortunate child of the Buddhas: by connecting
the profound oral instructions to the lineage of accomplished
practice, the result, present from the start, becomes manifest—
doubts and efforts are laid to rest and like a carefree tiger you
roam the jungle of awareness appearance.

The expanse of awareness is without inner or outer.
The expanse of wisdom is without clarity or obscuration.
The expanse of dharmadhatu is pervasive.
The expanse of the Great Bindu is beyond transition.
The expanse of experience is without interruption.

Well, there you go, love.

62.

The Buddhahood of Mind itself.
The Buddhahood of Mind itself.
The Buddhahood of Mind itself.

Mind appears one way. But mind is a trickster. Unborn wisdom mystery puts on the clothes of this and that thought, identity, form and says, "Fooled you!" Mind's functioning implies separation of self and appearance, mind and body, subjects objects but then mind's functioning is a liar.

On a cloudy day the sky looks grey but up above the clouds it is always blue. From the ground the moon seems to wax and wane but in the moon's own self experience there is only one big round globe. Mind seems to be born and die in accord with its movements and stillness but in truth it is one large open expanse of knowing's possibility.

The Buddhahood of Mind itself. Yeah, yeah you've heard it before from every Tom, Dick and Harry village Lama who went on to try and con you out of your money, get in your pants, require endless sycophantic kiss-assness (which you were eager to offer in your exchange of Catholic Guilt Shame Based Fear Religion for a new Asian flavor of same) and so it seems a worn and tired, almost cliché. But if you toss out your strategies and corruption then you will swiftly forget the shell game of most religionists and begin to take seriously the way.

It is a cliché but still, it is true. Mind itself is Buddhahood! Mind itself is Buddhahood!! Mind itself is Buddhahood!!! Take a deep breath, dust yourself off and reconsider everything. Take off the facade of past efforts and strip naked of the presumed understandings. Shake off the dreary sorrow of encounters with false priests born from one's own false intentions. There is a path whose nobility and beauty outshine all falseness. It is offered freely and, while it does require intelligence, hard work, and discipline it is also joyous, uplifting and beautiful.

A Tibetan friend told me this joke. "What does it take to become a Lama in America? A red robe and a passport." Still, this sad truth does not need to become the limit of your efforts. Where one's intentions and effort are authentic authenticity will manifest in the form of one's teacher; and, while spirituality tends to devolve into business in the climate of human culture, that is not its (or your) limit. Mind is, in fact, in its deep essence, nature, energy—Buddhahood itself waiting for you to realize it.

63.

The sweet slip away: part 1 The Freedom Place

A little child secure in his mother's love fearlessly ventures forth
like a rushing river.
A thousand sutras in my heart but my mouth has only
Silence.
There is a flare before the leaves fall away, crimson mountains
signaling winter's coming.

I found an old scrap of paper, behind a book, on my top shelf. On
the front were these words, written in my own hand, at some time
I no longer remember

> *Forgetting original food. We eat corpse meat.*
> *Forgetting original drink we gulp poison.*
> *Like a dandelion seed in the wind there is*
> *No knowing where "this" will land. No one to take "its hand."*
> And so: *The sweet slip away begins.*
>
> *The last sound to pass these lips will be "I love you"—*
> *but with no "i" no "you" no word like "love."*

An old man sits on his porch after a long day's work. Tired
bones of everything settled deep in a chair while evening sun
slants across pine decking, bright fades to black, ease enters like
a welcomed guest. He is whistling a tune whose words I can't
remember but whose title I do—"The Sweet Slip Away."

Sky puts on cloud robes and my mind is high low like sunlight.
Appearances abound and the freedom place pervades, the way
wetness pervades a drop of water. Clouds gone, stainless sky.
Sometimes it is hard to recall the old friends but I do remember

that renunciation begins the day we are born and finds perfection on the day we die.

A river rushes through my heart; the rushing is my heart and "through" is not a place. The river is called "Love's Gesture" and it pours out past appearance into an ocean named "Unborn." This river has a source, and this source has a name. It is called The Freedom Place.

Appearances swim like little fishies in the deep of the Freedom Place—galaxies, universes, countless beings and Being. Run your hand through the velvet blackness and the water will shine—"The disciple enjoys the manifold fruits while the Guru rests within easeful freedom."—Kabir.

A little child secure in his mother's love fearlessly ventures forth like a rushing river. A thousand sutras in my heart but my mouth has only Silence. There is a flare before the leaves fall away, crimson mountains signaling winter's coming.

64.

Up at 4:30 AM, the freezing cold has returned in the night, almost down to zero. Walking across the field ice crystals cling to branches and the moon's light dances over them turning the entire vista into sparkling diamonds. White is an expanse of love. Dark tree branches are the emblem of wonderment and the crunch of snow under foot is the declaration of Buddhahood. To see this way (and I do not mean as an idea but literally—a physically different way of knowing) is to be free from violence, alienation, dull sorrow.

Outwardly the world has become the insignia of beauty. Inwardly the world has become the liquid pulse of love. This is what is meant by "tulku" or Nirminakaya—the incarnation of truth, beauty, goodness. This is what the mystic St. Symeon meant when he said, "I move my hand it becomes the whole of Christ." Secretly the world is simply what it has always been.

There is no elation in this perception. There is no hype, no high. It is simply the natural state of the body, mind, feelings trained to their full capacity. It is the birthright of every being but also the being obligation debt of every person. If this manner of seeing, living, is not realized then one's life has not flowered and there is dissatisfaction. Where no "self" mediates between the divine and appearance then the flowering is complete and beauty, truth, goodness incarnates. This incarnation is the divine purpose of human existence.

The ear meets with the sound of the morning birds and there is no thought, no movement, only mystery of sound in Silence. This is Buddha's speech. Eye meets with the crystal diamond light of frost and there is no thought, no movement of mind, only the bliss of color and light in empty space. This is Buddha's sight. Legs moving, grasses brushing pants leg, and there is no thought, no movement of mind—motion becomes joy and joy spreads as love. This is the activity of the Bodhisattvas.

Movement, sight, sound all have become the Beloved. This is beyond argument and disputation, proofs and syllogisms. Twenty-one years now this body has been lived in-as-through-of this. Waking, dreaming, deep sleep—no change. In this empty purity and luminous clarity body becomes the act of Love, the art of offering.

Profound Immensity!!!!! Wu Shi—Nothing special.

Sun, sky, field, hill—the contours of my beloved's face. Perception and sensation—warmth of her touch. Here, Oh yogi, there is no fretful conflict between the divine and appearance—no duality, only display. Here in the palace of unstained bliss celestial dancers of ceaseless delight cavort and frolic like stars—playful under the light of the wisdom moon.

65.

The vast wisdom bliss of Buddha manifests in forms of sensual beauty, light and sound. These images and mantras cause a sympathetic resonance in the mind drawing you toward wisdom-bliss. This is the compassionate action of the Buddhas.

∾

Devotion is the natural love response to what is most beautiful. If a tuning fork pitched to middle C is tapped it will resonate with the single note. If it is brought close to another tuning fork not tapped, not resonating, the untapped one will begin to resonate as well. This is called sympathetic resonance. Devotion is the resonance in feeling to what is divine.

∾

Silence is like a deep ocean undisturbed by any event. Silence lives in and as the silent mind. Love is like the vast open sky embracing all appearances impartially. Love lives as the awakened heart. Love and Silence are the stronghold of the realized one and the inheritance of every being.

∾

The mind is universal but if it is limited to the small size of the body then how can it function properly? Sense of body is also universal—all life a single body, this is the natural feeling of reality. But if limited to single "body-self" how can compassion blossom? It is a question of coming to know who you truly are.

66.

It is useless to try and ease hunger by reading the menu or endlessly discussing recipes—one must eat the meal. To propagate spiritual concepts is simple and of no great import. When you become hungry you will order the food and eat. When longing in the heart goes beyond the superficial then you will take up the way and bring the mind from the unnatural to the natural.

∽

The unborn nature of reality does not deny appearance it only denies birth. Awareness does not "pervade" space; the radiance of awareness is space and it is the play of appearance within space. The play of appearances is itself substanceless intangible wisdom. Nothing else.

∽

Beyond notions twoness or oneness, my Heart dyed in the color of Love and Silence stands at the threshold of emptiness and form filled with invitation. This stronghold of the realization is unassailable, immaculate, blameless. From this placeless place all appearance is the gesture of love. The offering given from deity to deity without the slightest trace of notion—giver, receiver or gift.

67.

A prayer to Manjugosha, Lion of Speech[1]

I bow down to the Guru who is only kindness, peace and protection:

DHIH! Affectionate One, who shines like the bright sun, Manjushri, father of Buddhas, please grant your blessing dispelling obstructions.

Foremost amongst the children of Buddha, Manjushri, great Lion of Speech, please grant that my voice will carry your power.

Red in color and wielding a sword, Manjushri, conquering hero,please scatter the clouds' endarkening wisdom.

Great gem of knowledge, whose mind is all brightness, Manjushri, Arapachana,[2] Please grant that my mind be swift and unhindered.

Manjushri, Lord of Knowledge and Speech, child of the Buddha Amitabha, to you I pray from my heart. Grant that the eight treasures, enriching the stronghold of my mind, be firm and that my speech become like the roar of the Dharma dragons.[3]

---

[1] Manjugosha = Gentle Voice

[2] Arapachana = a name of Manjushri

[3] 8 treasures of great strong mind = 1. Intelligence 2. Recollection 3. Realization 4. Memory (retaining the teachings) 5. Confidence 6. Possessing dharma 7. Bodhicitta 8. Accomplishment

OM AH RA PA CHA NA DHIH

*At the repeated request of Tsochen Khandro, a pure-
hearted Dakini, I, Tulzhug Pawo, wrote down these words
for my friend Boone, who hides the brightness of wisdom
within his mind. Through confidence in the Buddha's
power and truth may its syllables remove the clouds of
obscuration and cause the sun of wisdom to shine across
the expanse of space.*

*Dakini Day, month of the Full Flower Moon, 2010: May all
beings be happy!*

68.

It's not outside! It's not inside!

Quick! Right now death has you in its sights, finger on the trigger.

1. Buddha, Lao, Jesus, Krishna long dead. Right now the very same mind that animated them abides within you. Dabbling in sadhana, shallow curiosity, half -hearted efforts can't awaken this sleeping giant. Question the authority of your identifications, opinions, superstitions.

2. When mind is full of contradictions then perception becomes dull and mind projects worry, fret, nervousness, self-concern onto light and shadow, tree branch, sounds in the forest at night. Self-concern occludes, like cataracts on the eyes, the simple presence of freedom and beauty within mere appearance.

3. The straight jacket of Point of View, the dull temerity of birth and death, the superstition of subject and object all join the brouhaha patriotism of mind's ceaseless conceptualizing.

How sad to live not having known, cultivated, brought to flowering, the longing of the Heart. Uncorrupted by birth, death, thought, self, other, confusion, suffering, there is a stainless jewel within the Heart. Be still and know this mystery.

69.

There are five tall poles outside my hut, once they carried prayers on the wind. Tattered long ago, smudged bits of cloth now.

My life. This old rusted machine, a dishwasher, fridge, old car tossed over the edge, into deep ravines down the gulley over on Dennison Rd., West Virginia's recycle center.

(You can't just roll those heavy ones off the truck either. It takes two men to lift, tug, draggggg it away. Ignominious goodbye to what once served you well, now replaced by this year's fashion. No backyard burial next to the goldfish, beside the hamster, the beloved cat whose hair lingers around the house. There is no child's play headstone, no bouquet of posies—just rusted metal in the damp wood, my old life.)

Maybe February comes and goes in the midst of other months. Maybe sarcasm, like fog, creeps in on little cat's feet making a shadow puppet bargain of flesh on flesh. Maybe life is a book fallen from the library shelf, fallen shut.

Twilight erases every thing, undoes the doing of our day. No one misplaces twilight. No one misses the infinite shades of dissolution, forgetting the mystery they offer.

I made a shadow puppet on the wall, I called it my life. A luminous branch shines in rays of light through mist, early morning, 5 AM

perfect.

Sentient beings are born and die. Bodhisattvas emerge And dissolve. Buddhas never move from totality. Oh friend: let the mind serve its true purpose.

Sitting side by side on this park bench there is love and in this shirt there is nothing but the tenderness of new dawn.

70.

There is no separation in the moonlight's love affair with the pine.

Headlights break the edge of hill and a thousand times a thousand rays of brilliance explode the panorama of darkness. Green trees, a red brick edge, the line of a telegraph pole emerge as emptiness' form and love fills mind with mystery. Walking in the hot summer night, 2 AM, there is a sense of pregnant stillness and immense power filling world.

The patterns of leaves shift in the breeze and on the horizon the blue-black clouds churn and roil, an occasional flash of lightning breaking the dark. Soon the summer thunderstorm will arrive with its fury and winds like God's own gardener pruning the weak and dead branches of the woods. Sometimes this destructive force is needed. Sometimes compassion must wear the mask of wrath to clear the old and stagnant and, in the decomposition of fallen branches, new soil, new life, will be born.

Furious winds blow against the narrow confines of confusion breaking the rigid structure of ego's lock-and-key mentality. Suddenly un-guessed vistas open. A moment's love gathers compassion's cloudbank releasing summer's rainfall. Life, like droplets of light, fall from nowhere into everywhere. Who will set aside the politics and bartering of ego's every whim, preference and opinion and stand in the strong wind and rain. There is discomfort in the storm and also renewal. One must be willing to bear the discomforts of the work to come to a rebirth, a transformation in consciousness.

There is a secret in the body, pathways of light and joy encased in the rigid encrustations of a thousand million years of habit. It will take a strong blow to crack the prison walls and allow sunlight to enter the dark cave of isolation. The first large drops of hot rain have begun to fall. Suddenly the sky is illuminated by brilliance and thunder cracks open the world.

The ink of appearances writes the story of awakening on the pages of existence. Life, nature, all experience is living symbol, an open book on "the way." Learning to read this book is the import of the work. The wind is gusting and the air is filled with the fresh scent of new growth.

71.

18. See David Bohm, **Wholeness and Implicate Order**. *Concerning the implicate order the author said (p.149): "This order is not to be understood solely in terms of a regular arrangement of* **objects** *(for example in rows) or as a regular arrangement of events (for example in a series). Rather, a* **total order** *is contained, in some* **implicit** *sense, in each region of space time."*

—Herbert Guenther, *The Creative Vision*, footnotes

rlung-smyo, insane by virtue of the wind:

brilliant moon   hidden harmony   the fact of
palatial mansions

standing in the rain 2:30 am   archaic
heartbreak flower fingertip old memory new place
                              a
                              n
                              d
                              the invariance of
Being's urge dims down ....

          egological premises egological concern
constrict, and Love can not,

                                   t
                                   u
                                    r
                                   n   this
moment
                         around again.

72.

Hexagram 37 Dwelling People: (if you took the sum of my words they would indeed spell the name of G-d)

Rutilated quartz. Dis-appropriate entanglements in the hour of our departure. I turn to the poppy, its ability to unravel time, its red petals, delicate stem. I turn to Borges, who stands beside me whispering something unheard, unhearable. I turn toward twelve sisters who guard the hours of day and night.

I turn outward to meetings and inward toward moonlight. My fingers almost touch the edge of an impossible notion. I turn toward supraluminal blueness. I count my ancestors.

Consciousness has missed its import, mediated as it is by identification creating individuality. It has lost the page on which was written a mysterious intersection of all and everything, nothing and no-thing. It has fallen over the edge of Silence. I remember my grandfather's cigar smoke, the feel of a leather playing card case, my grandmother's roses.

Beyond impossibility is appearance. Beyond comprehension is the number 9, a cat's stalking walk, sudden exclamations of color from the random meeting of raindrops and eyeglasses and knees go weak inside the transient loveliness of sunlight.

There is no world, no self, no Point of View. There is no wanting, no having, no being …. and thus tenderness is introduced to somethingness. Love is born. There is a country for appearance. I turn again to Borges, his lips form words, sound travels the impossibility of distance and I hear the word . . . .

73.

..... a single thought of love and this old shirt fills with
warmth, worn cuff, one button missing,

> soft with days and nights.

If I could share the indescribable beauty discovered in
perception when mind is gone to Silence there would be
no more violence, no more alienation.

> This longing.
> The communicative thrust of joy.
> The afterthought of luminosity.

> This
>
> mind without form,
> form without limit,
> no need for the extraordinary.

74.

Spiritual silence, a fullness of divine possibility, is a meaning-saturated field in which life inheres, rises falls, like waves on the ocean. This knowing gives birth to expression, a song of joy whose notes spread the filament of truth, beauty and goodness across the interrelatedness of life.

To discover this one cannot numb the mind with dogmas, with mechanical systems—which never was the import of the spiritual path but merely ego's co-opting of it. The path must be walked in a manner organic and alive. Each step follows from the birth of an ever-fresh and new understanding. Even while the path and the methods strip away mechanical conditioning, one must be careful that it itself not become yet another mechanical conditioning.

Sitting on the edge of my bed, 3 AM—a dog's bark, the sound of a raccoon scurrying, the breeze through the forest leaves, all of this deepened the immensity.

A harmonious order filled the whole of life and was itself held within the dimension of sacredness and silence. Sanctity, silence and harmony were one and the same thing and the motions of life enhanced rather than disturbed this purity.

Life itself is held within this harmony the way the baby Jesus was held by the hands of Mary. Sitting, perfectly still, feeling spreads across knowing as silence and love. It was as if the fretful business of human concerns had paused to allow knowing of infinite blessedness, life as the breath of living spirit. This pause has now gone on 20 years now.

The brain must have deep rest from the conditioning of thought. When it does then harmony permeates body and world. The methods of the path do not "create" this rest, they remove the habit of frantic distraction and undo the deformities in body and feeling born from decades of confusion and hurt. The harmony is uncreated, natural, spontaneous and uncorruptible. It is always present yet seldom seen for it is covered, missed due to distraction.

Outside the barking of a coyote pack signals death for some creature. Nature, of itself, is filled with both horror and wonder. A night bird calls. All of this is held within inviolable purity. Knowing is inseparable from the coyote, its prey, the night air, and it is also something more. Knowing, arisen from spiritual silence and fullness, moves in through as appearance as the affectionate peace of the unborn wisdom mind of Buddha.

The nearly full moon shines and its rays touch leaves, earth, the water of a stream. The moonlight reflected in water, the unborn harmony reflected in mind. The breeze carries the scent of old leaves and wet earth.

75.

there is nowhere to hide everything)
     naked mind   subtle light
               curve
    and eloquence on the threshold of empty   space.

Mind stripped bare contains no (con)venient *is*
or *is not*, no nest, no den, no place to rest one's
head. Conceptless clanking of cooking pots is
homeless. The sound of speech in a market
place, the sonata of random sound.

structureless luminosities—five skandhas
empty from the beginning   are freedom.

A vine climbs a trellis:
                no birth   no death
           no sickness

                  no old age and death
          end of suffering   no suffering
             climbing

right on up to your honeysuckle lips, the moon of your
nails, the sway of your hips, twilight of your unreason,
arc of thigh and beauty of your nothing special
love   plenitude and emptiness   naked
mind   subtle light
      curve and eloquence.
                      (and

76.

mythologizing diction, import of birth and death,
suspicion that there may be another way   of viewing
the problem domain   called

. . . .   "being human."

silence is Being's thrust toward optimization,
undermining, unmaking

        the bounded domain of reason's either or

the proposition implies one of two answers:
the proposition, formed as a question   is   wrong.

you can not get a right answer to a wrong question.

babies are not born
old people do not die

there is no sweet hello and no sad goodbyes and yet . . .
just this moment,   your face,   my hand . . . .
the delicate beauty
                        of impermanence.

77.

Hand moves across beam, 140 years old, rough, hand-hewn, a foot thick walnut, born from a labor filled with patience and love. The old barn is filled with history, timber and chocolate wood's rich memory. The setting sun's rays filter through the west wall and make patterns of light across the pine floor. The warm fall evening is filled with barn swallows swooping and the songs of dahlias. Two swallows torment the cat laying on the driveway, swooping close to her head only to fly away at the last second as the paw lashes out. The cat rises, stretches, and slips into the garden to stalk through lettuce and broccoli.

Body and heart gone to bliss and settled in wisdom remember Pablo Neruda's line: "I love you with out knowing how, or when, or from where." Mind rested in silence recalls Zen Master Bankei saying, "The more you move into truth the deeper it is." Human beings fear aloneness and so they will not allow mind and heart to journey into the vast unknown places of mystery where the depths Bankei speaks of are found. To remain in the known is to stagnate.

To be alone you must be free to question everything, free to leave behind memory, knowledge, information. There is tremendous sensitivity in leaving behind everything. In insecurity the mind, the body, the feelings become delicately aware. The pulse of perception, free from even the notions perceiver and perceived, dissolves into the pattern of life and there is no isolation. To be alone you must first leave behind conditionings and then leave behind even the notion "I." For this the muscles associated with the interface between body and mind must be made keenly strong—this is the work of the spiritual path.

True intelligence is born in a mind free from the conditionings of knowledge and awake in the process of knowing. Pseudo Dionysius, a fifth century Christian mystic, spoke of Luminous Ignorance. The pure knowing of awareness has no collection of knowledge, no bits and pieces of the past—only a pure knowing in the immediacy of perceiving. Information is stored in the brain but has no true place in the mind of awareness.

Here in the barn, perception stretches out as world in the Original Hermitage, time's smallest measure. Here the notion "Buddha" or "being" mean nothing at all. Eternalism, nihilism, dualism, monism are forgotten like the wrapping on a child's Christmas present. The sun shining against the red of barn is living flame playing in subtle hues and colors. On the western horizon the evening star shone with brilliant clarity.

78.

Do you know . . . .
the flavors of sunrise, eye meeting form, lover meeting love? Have
you known the silent way light moves from heart to eye to form
the world from a stuff far more wondrous than dreams?

Do you know . . . .
the dark twig, the pine's shadow and how damp forest soil tastes
to the soul? Have you known spring's greening of life deep into
the marrow, the fields, pastures, plains of body's landscape?

Do you know . . . .
the way ear meets sound, old friend, new love, fragile first kiss?
Have you known bird calls, the cry of a baby, the sound of an
engine, rested in mind's vast space, known as Love only?

Do you know . . . .
the corpses of casual disregard, the wounded heart torn by unlove?
Have you known the shipwrecks of this life's efforts, the taste acrid
in the mouth, the sharp crystals of reason?

Do you know . . . .
The scar of isolation, the hornet of alienation's repeated sting?
Have you known a thousand shattered pieces of dawn, sun meeting
dark sky, spread out across your day with the cold of no regret?

Do you know . . . .
the immaculate touch that restores mind and heart?
Have you known the dreaming dark knowing with its mysterious
tiny-ness of all moments—so small they engulf the world.

79.

One short pause between
the leaky road here
and the never leaking Way there:
If it rains let it rain!
If it storms let it storm!
>   —Zen Master Ikkyu

Awareness has no center, circumference, origin, location, point of view. It is simply function, the function of knowing without there being any "one" who knows. When the radiant knowingness mistakes its knowing for a subjective entity who "knows" then it also mistakes appearances for objective entities that are known.

Awareness is the bright functioning of a perfect mystery. What makes it perfect is that it is not only unknown but unknowable. You can be it but you can never know it. You can discover you are it but you can never understand it as "it" is beyond knowing or understanding. It is perfect mystery. Awareness is the bright functioning of this perfect mystery.

Appearances are the dreams of awareness just as, at night, dreams of the human being are nothing other than the dreamer. Appearances are nothing other than awareness. Dreams arise in human consciousness. Appearances arise in awareness. Awareness is the bright functioning of a perfect mystery. Appearances and awareness are not two nor are they one—they are just mysterious, beyond birth, death, self, other, location or substance.

When awareness does not recognize that it is the function of a bright mystery and has no "location" or subjective entity "self," then it also forgets appearances are only its own dreaming. Just as the dreamer forgets their dreams are themselves. Awareness now needing a location in which "to be," clothes itself (the mistaken notion of being a subjective entity) in appearances. Immediately it identifies itself perfectly with its clothing of body and place—embodiment and enworldment.

This is a cramped view, to say the least. How can that which is birthless and deathless exist happily in the constraint of smallness? The subtle intuition of previous freedom is always nagging somewhere deep in the mind, heart and body.

It is in response to this nagging discomfort that the strategies of life arise in an attempt to find release from suffering. There is no solution to dream problems within the dream, only in awakening.

Once you know there is no solution within the mechanics of the problem then life becomes substantially simpler and waking up becomes your interest.

80.

Bliss.
Sudden.
Open like the sky.
Arises as infinite shimmering light display.

Bliss.
Overwhelming.
Deep like the ocean.
Arises from the play of emptiness and action.

Bliss.
Simple.
Like the singleness of empty clarity.
Present without striving without contrivance.

No goal,
No frustration,
Not two, not one, not none.
Mind of space and form, mind of Master and disciple,

Deep night, pines sway, moon.
Beauty fills the sky and in a single glance,
all at once, the path of no more learning.

81.

Buddhism, when you reach its very depths, is like a man who knows nothing of Buddha or Buddhism.

　　　　　　　　　　　　—Zen Master Takuan

Perceiving is deity.
What is perceived is the wisdom mandala.
The mind that perceives is sunyata
(emptiness/mystery).

Come to rest as the immovable nothingness of this sunyata mind and you will "know" nothing of Buddha or Buddhism but you will be inseparable from Buddha and Buddhism. When mind stops at "Buddha"—Buddha dies. When mind again returns to its natural state where this is no partiality, no wisdom, no delusion, no birth, no death, no path, no bondage, no enlightenment, no sentient beings, no Buddha—then Buddha flourishes.

To train the mind to naturalness, which means to unlearn the unnatural (and this can be very hard work as the habits or unnaturalness are embodied and enworlded in our habit), is to bring the Buddha to life and, also, it is to forget the Buddha.

"Glancing at something and not stopping the mind is called *immovable wisdom,* as the heart is filled with various judgments, this is movement within and the mind stops. When this movement ceases then the mind that has stopped moves, but it does not move at all. It is immovable."—Zen Master Takuan

The mind is pervasive immovable wisdom. It is pervasive because it extends through and as space instantly. Having moved to the extent of space it is immovable. When it stops on this or that object, identifies with it in some manner, or fills itself with the movement of judgment/thought, then its function is obscured. Instead of effortlessly moving through appearance, as the womb space *of* appearance, it becomes fixed, fixated.

Oddly it is precisely when the mind stops that it ceases to be immovable. Mind stops when it becomes grasped by the logic of partiality; mind stops, is held up in its perfect extent, and becomes the smallness of the "now" and the "here." Don't even "be here now," don't be any "where" or "when," don't even "be"—all of these are the mind stopping. Simply do not interfere in the marvelously illuminating function of unborn awareness.

When mind rests in immovability then every thing and everything is known perfectly, easefully in its naturalness and emptiness. Then mind remains free in appearances, unmoving, never stopping.

82.

In this old tattered womb bag of emptiness
MindHeart circles without boundary or circumference
eating the meal of all appearance.

In the Chevy backseat love parlor of Being
BodyMind joins the orgy of sunlight and pattern
and birth is the inevitable result of love.

In this form realm world of spinning emptiness
AwarenessAppearance watches its father slip away in
Ernest Hemingway-look-alike death.

Unrecognized in three worlds I do not even know my
own name anymore. Wandering wayside paths, neither
yogi nor bhogi, just a fool who once knew so much and
now has unlearned even the act of knowledge.

Simplicity's bright joy, dark knowing's deep mystery
and down at the Northside Grill they are cooking up
caramel nut rolls for breakfast. Old Joe will be sitting
in the back telling his war stories and across the street
kids play in the park.

In this world—shape-shifting congenial friend.
In that world—display of luminous clarity.
In truth, neither this nor that—mostly just heartbroken.

83.

Rinpoche could you please explain this line of Longchenpa: "Space, as manifest design of Being's nothingness, shackles all within its iron grasp." Her question was asked with such innocence; her being lacked all trace of guile. Without expectation or grasping we sat in the silence of the question neither of us moving toward contrived answers. Without thought or effort speech began:

Dynamic nothingness is the ground of all phenomena, it is the sourceless beginningless source, beginning, and ever present reality, of everything and every thing. There is no where or when or why that is other than this dynamic nothingness. Its own nature is an expanse of knowingness and this cognitive force tosses out its ownmostness as the expanse of "space." This space is not the "space" that is a container for appearances—that is the mistaken notion of subjectivity. This space is just wide openness, a playful illusion of dimensionality where the luminous radiance of nothingness—its dynamism—can cavort. The pure cognitive intensity of nothingness' dynamism tosses dimensionality out the way an artist lays down a sheet of paper. Then it takes the luminous clarity of its nature, like a multi colored ink, and writes secret scripts, makes meaning-full symbols called all appearance.

There is one ground, two paths, two results. The one ground is the dynamic nothingness. What I call the Nothingness State. The dynamic quality of this nothingness, that is not a mere emptiness but a state of perfect potential, displays its potential as the seeming actualization of space, realms, worlds, beings. The first of two paths is that the cognitive intensity of knowingness/awareness does not forget that all is its own play. Then there is simply appearance as Nothingness' illusion clothing. The second state is one where the true nature of appearance is forgotten and awareness becomes individuated consciousness within the realm, on a world, as a being— believing in its own reality the way a character in a dream believes in the reality of the dream.

In the first, the body is both part and whole at one and the same time; and beyond this it is the Nothingness State. It participates perfectly, totally, and yet is free in, and as, at the same time. In the second the body is seemingly trapped in its own small container of flesh, world, Being. Then "space" as the complimentary concept to "Being" is the prison of Beings . . . .

The talk went on for some time, back and forth. Because her mind was free from any stain, the words were met with the understanding born of perfect clarity. One body's ability to speak meaning was met by another body's ability for uncomplicated understanding and so there was tremendous joy in our play-full conversation.

In all circumstances all conversation is, in fact, conversation between Buddha Nature and Buddha Nature. Sometimes it is even realized.

84.

She is a fabulous Being—half human,
half drum, flute and symbol.
(an orchestra of erotic Realism)

Hips of invitation, heavy with joy,
alive with knowledge and the Freedom of delight.
> *Not pornography but iconography
> describes that liquid motion.*
Across the sky of mind, her touch rings like a turquoise bell
transforming the bandits of passion, healing wounds of flesh
and memory long forgotten, lost in deep places of earth.

Caverns of lineage teaching form her belly, a deep navel
birthplace of Buddhas. Her neck is a swan—the great
Paramahansa, and her every word—a secret script
All in All a constellation of happiness.

For twelve hundred years I have been lost to the smile
of those hips—the hidden ground of primordial wisdom.

> *Since that day, I find in the motion of
> love and form and body not the tired end of
> desire or fretful consolation but the pulse of
> living, a deep moss scent of life, a wild blue
> gesture out beyond One or Two*

In each naked moment our living arises without correction or
distraction.

This is the natural yoga of spontaneous joy.
> *Her eyes were the way of open sky,*

Whatever arises—instantly known as Emptiness Brightness,
that delicate color of compassion, and filled

here without contemplation or without effort.
me with the wild clarity of joy and then entered

Unobstructed, primordially pure, our own original nature
me into a forest of primeval humor.

is the union of perception and delight.

85.

foot, thigh, breastlaughtercurve and smile.)

Dark cloud cavorts with sky, expectant earth waits for
rain.   And the intimations of greening   a joy
announced

                                     symbol of the unborn.

What would you say to her? This woman whose
emptiness presence invites the Silence of mind.

If she were to ask "Where do you come from?" How
would you answer?

Would you speak of ocean stirrings? Would you show
her, as answer, the tools of manual labor, the path
through a prairie, unremembered trails of violets?
Would you mention the hunter, the farmer, the
furrowed brow of nocturnal questions and long
voyages? Would your fingers touch the keyboard and
reveal Chopin's Nocturnes?

But she did not ask. She sang and her song revealed all
that and words, unrecognizable words, words in
the foreign tongue of birthless and deathless joy:

I am the one who is empty yet full,
I am the one who is silence and song.
I am the celibate whose body is the act of love.
I am the formless who is all form.

Your body is existence and what you do not find there will
not be found. Mind is a flowing of its currents, without

base or substance. The body is an ocean of feeling, a
sacrifice and a joy.   *(the burden of Love)*

The body is a glorious city,
labyrinth and syntax,
the 24, the 16!

The flavors of feeling, the milk of the lion, the twining of
the creeper—Spontaneity in Stillness.

With the first flush of love she appears. The Generous
One, vivid symbol and dance. She is wider than the sea
and all   appearances are the islands of her
love.

Loving is a passage with no other shore . . . .

And so, now this inheritance: Perception becomes
freedom. Action becomes delight.

                    (and with the first flush of love

86.

I followed the streambed down the mountain. Large boulders glistened and, in some places, the moss was several inches thick. Lush, inviting. Lying down on a large boulder covered in thick leaves and moss there was a cathedral of patterns, light and shadow, amongst the leaves. A paw paw, with fruit the bears had not yet found, was directly overhead. The smooth roundness of their shape against a fragment of blue sky was achingly beautiful.

To see beauty but not allow mind to grasp, to long for ownership, is a deep secret of freedom. To remain purely present, without any contrived notion of the "now"—without any concept spiritual or worldly—is to dissolve in the perceiving action. Where does this perceiving come from? From a vast of pure mystery. Where does it abide—in a display of pure mystery. A mystery that is beauty—lived in body, feeling, mind. A beauty flowering in spontaneous action unstained and free. The origin of all art, the urge to beauty's creation, comes from moments of such perception.

All perceiving is rooted in emptiness, non-identity, but conception so swiftly claims ownership that the intrinsic beauty is crushed by the aggression of secondary, always fretful on some level, states. When the mind has re-learned its natural state then perceiving is simply allowed to function within space and beauty is known again. Recognized (re-cognized). Perceiving itself is known to be the only deity. What is perceived is the wisdom mandala of delight and the mind which perceives is the Nothingness State of no-identity.

Following the stream on down to the river there were two men fishing in a small boat. Their cooler of beer was open and both were smoking. The acrid smell of pot wafted across the breeze. The narrow constriction of mind's dysfunctionality is a cause of pain and torment to the body. Most of life's energy is spent trying to medicate this feeling of torment. Once lost within the rounds and rounds of identification there is no solution to the problem within the problem. The space of the "me" is doomed to stagnation much like eddies of water trapped by a fallen tree and accumulating debris and pollution.

Behind me the rich moss life of the woods was filled with silence and sound. Rhododendron were beginning to bloom. The sound of running water interrupted the radio music from the boat and invited play. A bed of moss awaited and the possibility, if this lies very still, of seeing the bear.

87.

Remembering Pseudo-Dionysius the Areopagite:

In the gloaming hour, when intimations of twilight steal
past the guardians of reason,   the   forest of
               unreason   beckons w
                                                    i
                                                    t
                                                    h its
language of bird song

stories the color of blood, and
the impracticable murmur of breezes.   Footsteps
                                          t
                                          r
                                          a
                                          v
                                          e
                                          l across the
landscape of

syllables, obscure ceremonies, and
mind's luminous expanse.

Here in the twilight hour of my undoing, whole parades
of concept are undone, left, scattered across the floor
like so much discarded wrapping paper. Unmade by
luminous unknowing's love. Tear the shirt of raison
d'être, rend the shackles of "because" and enter the
kingdom of forgetfulness.

88.

Many things we need can wait. The child cannot. Now is the time his bones are formed, his mind developed. To him we cannot say tomorrow, his name is today.

—Gabriela Mistral

The cliffs of the Val D'enfer had inspired Dante in his description of hell and so it gained this name, Valley of Hell. The stone, carved into phantasmagorical forms by eons of wind and rain, draws the mind into its twists and turns. The heat saturates the body and the insistent wind wears down the psyche's defense. So much beauty and mysticism has dwelled in this land of Provence, this wayfare of cultures and epochs.

During the summers of teen years the body, mind, spirit absorbed much from living in this land. Silent longing found expression in the crypt of Sara la Kali at Saintes Maries de la Mer. Meditation became expansive in the tiny ancient churches and at the Abbey de Senanque. The body knew joy and love in the lavender fields, walking through the mountains, floating on the Ardéche.

Down in the crypt of Sara la Kai silence had consumed mind's functions and living purity pervaded space. The body, 19 years old, was filled with unexplainable joy and stillness. An old gypsy man entered the crypt. He approached the statue of Sara, draped in many layers of beautiful cloth. She was dark and beautiful. The old man stood silent for some time and then slid his hand up under her dress fondling her smooth supple form, kissing her cheeks.

The intimacy of this act opened the silence like the blooming of a peony. The kisses of the ants, their feet wandering the bud unfold the petal, and his hands roaming her body, intimate like the lover he was, and his kisses so tender unlocked the power inherent within silent contemplation. Appearance is the great offering of emptiness' paradoxical fullness. The great offering of love into form, the incarnation of the divine. The whole of appearance. Without hesitation emptiness surrenders itself into form and form back into emptiness and in this love play everything and every thing is made, done, undone, unmade. Mind and body felt awe in witnessing the old gypsy's touch, caress, kiss and love. The boundaries of worldly and divine dissolved and countless lessons about the ways of love were learned.

Wandering outside there was a crowd on the beach. Walking down the shoreline and into the crowd there was the shock of seeing the bloated body of a drowned man that had washed up on shore. These two shocks, one after the other, changed that young man forever.

89.

In the kitchen circling the only love, a feast is prepared:

Longing lights the fire of sacred vows.
Stout-heartedness tenderizes the meat of body mind
While a single tear of love, like a whole fist of garlic and herbs,
spices the stew.

Cooked in the pot of devotion, mixed with the fruits and
vegetables of vision and sound, the savory broth
thickens. The aroma cascades in circles of steam
through the moments of life.

Heat fills the body kitchen. The fire of longing's pleasure
stoked high breaks open the hard shell of reasons fruit —
tasty juice of deathless joy pours over four kinds of
sweet cake. Ah, now that's a dessert!

Finally, the after dinner drink. Smooth as velvet, fierce
as fire, over the tongue and bright in the belly—rested
in the heart deep going nowhere—complete as one,
complete as two!

Our way is to offer our lives as a feast of love.

Prepare your feast well, my friend, for truly you are
what you eat!

90.

Rising from the Heart of Silence
Bright with birthlessness

a secret space above the head (right now reach your
arm straight up above your head and snap your fingers
—right there), at an impossible right angle to all
appearance, the light of mystery spins out forms of
every world

and everyplace

      everywhere

      everywhen   f

            a

      l

  l

    s

        when mind is freed, it falls.

It falls into the bowl of the sky. It falls to the origin
place. And there appearance experience hangs, like a
shirt on a hanger, on the chreods of configurational
space, that little mischievous prank of mind.

Enough of this fretful whirling dance of why and
Wherefore—this endless smashing of beauty by

because. Why not take a vacation out beyond
perception
where love dissolves all fear?
                    (let perception fall in droplets
                unencumbered by hope and fear)

Tell you what, I'll meet you there—drunk
and lost, every "thing" becomes everything!
I'll buy you dinner! I know the mâitre d'.
Jesus, at his usual table for twelve,
eats the meal of eternal sorrow and delight.
There's no buying or selling there no merchant
mentality of bargained salvation. You pay the bill
with the destruction of reasons. (excuses for the word
"No")
Lao Tzu plays sax in the band and
Buddhas dance a quick step.
Beyond knowledge, beyond Silence, beyond
the tedious round of births and deaths.

What'ya say—want to take a vacation?

91.

The rain had come. For days the sky grew blue-black like a bruise and the dry earth waited, longed. Now the wind had kicked up dust devils and grit, twigs, small pebbles flew about as the large heavy drops fell down onto the ground. In a few hours, when the winds had passed and the rain had saturated the earth, there would be a deep renewal. The withered leaves would once again be full and radiant; the smell of rich dampness would signal life's upsurging.

Walking up the road towards a turn, a child was riding wildly in the rain. There was no avoidance of the wet in him, only embrace, only rejoicing. He did not carry an umbrella or cover his head with his shirt. Hooting and hollering he built up speed and suddenly, raising his legs off the pedals, letting go of the handlebars, he coasted with a yelp of joy. Neither of us said a word to each other as he sailed by but he lit up the world with beauty and the meaninglessness of joy. The whole world smelled of innocence as if cunning had yet to be born.

Love is like the rain. It comes, unasked, in large drops, falling down on the ground of our spirit making everything fresh again. Psychological memory tends to stagnate the mind and heart. Memories of past hurts, pleasures, reinforce the habits of grasping and manipulation. If we can learn to shed this then we will receive the almost ceaseless gifts offered up by appearance's symbols. In the moment love comes, unbidden, unannounced, we must be tremendously alert—with the whole body. We need to be un-preoccupied. We need to be pre-unoccupied so that a climate of renewal, intimacy with life, can be known.

Intimacy lies in the immediacy of perceiving where perceived and perceiver have no distance. Then appearances move through us and us through them like planets in the single sky. This is possible when the brain and mind are trained to stillness. Not training as in conditioning but trained to total aliveness and rejection of those deadening tendencies that obscure.

The sun returned and patterns of light played across the alternating dark and bright, grey and blue, of the sky while the greening of new grass filled the mind and heart with joy. The boy, his bike forgotten in the grass beside the road, was running full tilt toward a tree.

92.

This is full; that is full.
From the full emerges the full;
Fullness coming from fullness, fullness still remains.
                    —Isa Upanishad

this line of sunlight traced to form   is no secret.
love is not hidden but exposed, vulnerable, in leaf,
twig, birth, death,
                    mothers, children, friendships.

announced from rooftop basement car horn whisper
. . . .   this line of sunlight

                    not born, will never die,
                    appears and disappears in
                    mystery   and   across

        pattern
        patterns
        patterning never ceasing magic.

The unborn does not deny appearances only birth and
so the born is born from the unborn while remaining
unborn.

                love   is required

to understand this unbirthing of reason's superstitious
assumptions;

the temptation of "is" and "is not," the seduction of
beauty by because
and even in failure

the tempest of flowers,
golden light on wheat fields,
barking dog, dark night   proclaim the victory of

unknowing.

93.

Tonight we dance in the temple of ruin,
our footsteps, like redundant circling,
mirror the heart and sky of lovesick birds.

Tonight we dance in the priory of new dawn,
our bodies prised open by longing's revelation,
magnolia blossoms on a hot summer's eve.

I want—(without shame or grasping fear)
the quick wings of your compassion.
the nakedness of your heart.

I want—the accumulation of syllables which dream red
like the blood of your loving.
I want—the reverie of hidden companions who
are called "the seducers of twilight."

I want—the mind, ever a tourist, in the ornament shop of your
Joy and the body, man in the desert thirsting for your presence.

Tonight we dance in the temple of ruin. For there is no hiding
from heartbreak, there is no running from messengers of sorrow
but, in the bright swell of your vast skyheartmind, all moments
submerge devoured by peace.

Tonight we dance in the temple of ruin,
laughter mixed with the broken
    tiles of my designs.

94.

Here in my little hut I am the richest man in the world.
Between heart and brow is a universe of happiness,
where love outshines all fear Drunken HeartMind
appearances dissolve into that which is unspeakably
real.

There is a dead vine on the fence, killed by winter and a
broken pot at the bottom of the stair. Where am "I"
now? What is "I"? No point to view, body as nexus of
mystery's presencing, space and color implied but not
garishly dogmatized.

Dynamic coherence, pattern and flow.
Appearance, implication, subtle curve and line.
Looked for the source and foundation cannot be
found. Just this looking and not finding is the
great secret. And yet, no one can deny its
appearance. Beyond the false of equation of "is"
and "is not" the simple facticity of mystery
silences the mind.

My Buddha nature? Your Buddha nature? ALL LIES AND
NONSENSE!
Simple awareness just as it is. The rest is only so much
garbage. If I had something, anything, I would give it
away. Having nothing I give that away too.

Free from implication body cavorts in the mytho-
poetics of appearing, language becomes the flow of
gnosemic structuring, mind holds a mirror up to itself
and sees the face of wonder.

95.

˙chos-kyi ying : an expanse of self revealing meanings

Erotic structures of sunlight do not intimate revolution.

Be a fool

> loss of mind crazy
> joy of heart—only
> > freedom.

> Indestructibility, intelligence.

Mind without form, form without location, and now the
royal household of body walks the street of the great
city without fear. Schematic diagrams of mystery's
unfoldment do not imply possible conspiracies,
malcontents with obscure names such as Birth or Death
never did lurk in hallways.

The architectonic process of becoming confuses the
resultant beings in fashions that cause said result to
search out cryptic outlines purported to inform mind of
freedom's whereabouts. Won't work.

The color blue invites mind out beyond the boundary of
reason.

Thematization antedates pattern, mind confounds
expanse with direction and meanings are isolated into
packets bought and sold. Aggregates are empty and so
bondage is liberated before it came into existence.

Postulated mysteries are mere opinion. Invited opinions on the nightly news are salesmanship lies offered Narcissus. Only four percent of people who send Tweets read anyone else's.

Cryptic explanation is engulfed in a garland of flame.

96.

Patterns of water droplets form a diamond blueprint across the old stump. Tiny ice jewels divulge mystery on the glitter of moss. The original tree has long since become humus and its soft spongy dirt, now under foot, has become home to new growth. In summer's heat tiny beetles and other insects dig tunnels, palaces and banquette halls in what remains—death becomes the stronghold of life. True dharma makes the mind stainless, uncorrupted, unconditioned and therefore tremendously sensitive.

Unburdened from erroneous concepts, propositions, and equations mind enters appearance freely, wholeheartedly, with tenderness. Appearance, with all its joy and sorrow, births and deaths, separation and loving, becomes the bible. It is not to be taken literally but as allegory, fable, symbol.

Everything is process; such pure process that there can be no nouns or adjectives in this sacred text of appearance. There are no 'things" or descriptions of the "static state" of "things." There are only verbs. The sky "is" not blue but it is blueing—and other times it is graying. There is no "tree" any longer, and life's moment of treeing has become, in the gloaming of this warm evening, the soiling, beetleing, homeing, fooding of life.

Being becomes. That is its joy. The love to be—free of fretful why and wherefore. Its inherent joy flowing out from the stronghold of divine mystery asks no reason or meaning. The mystery of emptiness and fullness becomes .... becomes, beetle, tree, sky, evening. It becomes human being and dog being and house and yard being. And it un-becomes, that daring process those impossible "things" called people call death.

Emptiness falls out itself as all appearance. The gesture of unrestrained loving. Appearance unmakes itself into emptiness. The affectionate surrender of infinite joy-fullness. Can mind be so delicate, so free from rigidity that it flows with the patterning and unpatterning without fear? Can it make no golden calf from name and forms, and let go the illusory boundary between being, becoming and the expanse of mystery.

The call of an owl has announced the dark. Held in stillness this motion of sound becomes disclosure of perfection in appearing, the inheritance of Buddhas. The smell of rich earth fills the night air.

97.

Biting the Tiger's Tail—advice from my dad on how to rise each morning:

My old man was born on a lotus and minced no words about it. One day he gave me some truly kick-ass advice. "Get out of bed and drop dead," he said. "Don't fret the small stuff, like birth and death"—

"But if I can't do that then........" (I whined)

"Well then, kid, you've gotta bite the tiger's tail. Grab her by her scruffy fur and jump up on her back. You've gotta shout 'Ya - Hoo' in the face of all appearance! Ain't no way around it—you've gotta swallow hope and fear like a pre-breakfast morning vitamin pill."

Drying off from the shower, shouting the mind splitting PHET— dharmakaya firecracker explodes the torment of mediocre timidity into a thousand spheres of rainbow. (Damn, I love that old man! What a teaching.)

Today, why not dress in clothes of no more cares? Trousers of great YES shouted into the heart of all events. Silk brocade of bliss realm presentation and regal hat of lineal grandiosity look nice when piercing the fabric of deluded concretization. Ahhhhh ... Of course, don't forget secret cloak of Dungdzin's power HUNG HUNG protector Dungdzin great black warrior with one face. (Perfect for power lunch deal making with cantankerous student.)

My old man was a Lotus Born Dharma hero. Certified grade "A" and he told me "Son, you've gotta kick some butt to survive the Dharma. You can't live in your world and in mine." Boy, he spoke it plain—no new age being of light macrobiotically channeled quick fix video chanting practice, bowing before cosmic cartoon edifice of personal limitation deity or pre-preliminary fantasy of eating cream filled ho-ho off belly of buxom sangha-mate, self glorifying guru yoga union with long dead movie star dharma king, psycho-babble pacification of childhood trauma dressed as Vajrasattva, endless internal quarrel with externalized daddy figure's challenging buffalo dance, humorless tasseled tit goddess grasping hope and fear new age soft core porn great vagina empowerment Dharma.

I'm talking cut the throat in one swift motion and drink the blood that's spilling from the aorta of delusion. I'm talking outlandish trans-cultural dharmakaya penetration Buddha nature idol of enlightenment smashed and left on conceptual landfill. I'm talking bliss-mad dance of Dakini blood drop realization. And I'm talking today—I'm talking 'bout biting the tiger's tail.

98.

In the airplane, above the clouds, there was the expanse of blue and the shining brilliance of the sun. Mind became quiet, concepts settled into their ownmostness—the always of unborn wisdom. Mind and space mingled and the body relished the sensations of silence in union with wonder. It is in such natural spontaneous meditation that mind is refreshed and made unstained by the past. This can not be bought or sold, created or controlled.

The Sufis say: "You can not come to enlightenment by following the path but only those who follow the path come to enlightenment." There is great truth in this that speaks to the imagined contradiction of the contrived nature of the path and the unconditioned freedom of reality. When the body is injured and crippled it is physical therapy that can restore its natural functioning. The exercises that restore are intentional, contrived, and yet it is their action that brings naturalness and functionality back. The exercises do not create the natural, they remove, repair, the obstacle.

The body, fat and lazy, cannot enjoy the naturalness of walking in the high mountains. Unnaturalness accustoms body and mind to unnaturalness. When this becomes habit, fixed in body feeling— thought, then the repair of this unnaturalness itself feels unnatural, difficult, contrived.

Looking out the window there was not a single thought. No movement in mind, heart and the body became still like a vast heavy mountain or deep ocean. There was peace beyond all contradictions such as birth, death, mine, yours. As peace grew beyond all limit the eyes closed and mind bathed in the eternity of silence.

Opening the eyes again after some unknown amount of time the hostess was standing with a drink; the sight of her caused the heart to surge with tender hearted affection born from stillness.

There are very few things that need thought. Thought restrained to its natural and appropriate functioning is a tremendous benefit. When it runs rampant across the territory of our lives, attempting to compensate for suffering with strategies, then it is the very origin of suffering. In the truth of a silent still mind feeling has only a few flavors and all of them are subtle variations of love. From the deep rest of mind eyes open, body encounters world, as the intentionless impulse of love.

99.

In the autumn chill a few remaining leaves cling to the trees. With each breeze more fall to the ground. Chaung Tzu, that enigmatic Taoist sage, once said, "When the shoe fits the foot is forgotten, when the belt fits the stomach is forgotten." When reality "fits," or better put, when body mind fit, ego's confusion and delusion is forgotten. The trees do not remember last spring's leaves.

Ego is not a "thing." Ego is not self-existent or static, it is an activity. It is the fretful activity of trying to make sense of existence based on false premises and faulty perceptions. When unborn wisdom awareness mistakes itself as the limit of consciousness flowing through particular body then the naturally arising frustrations of this tendency are the activity of ego.

The human system of mind, body, feeling is a single perceptual knowingness. A nexus of knowing comprised of synergistically functioning organs of perception. It is a moment of perceiving in an expanse of appearing. A wave on an ocean. The knowing and the appearing are the functioning of a marvelously bright and perfect mystery.

When the knowing and appearing mistake themselves for subject and object then the unworkable problem of ego arises. There is no answer to this problem situation called "human being." Ego is the activity of attempting to find the answer. The spiritual path is the realignment of the body, mind, feeling to perception without problem. When this is accomplished then quite naturally things are as they are. Within their momentariness they divulge the eternal. Within their partiality they disclose the whole.

Until this profound and natural reality is known in its spontaneous ease there will always be the attempt to find answers to problems that do not exist. The solution to the problem of death is found in relinquishing the imagination of birth. In awareness prior to consciousness.

A single leaf slowly falls to the ground. The shoe fitting, the foot is forgotten.

100.

Why did Rebbe Nachman go to Uman? To redeem the world. Why are you here?

—Dr. Kullman, Kenyon College

Eye to form is only love—without implication of being. Without problem of non-being. Free from dogma of perceiver or perceived.

The sky was blue and mauve, white with clouds and infinite like mind. A single crow, blacker than black, flew across its breadth. Mind was shattered into silence, its pieces scattered across the sea of meanings. Walking between the pines the smell of sap filled the nostrils. Perception is pure pleasure; the meeting of sense and sense field the enactment of primal love. Sometimes, suddenly, the whole body is made terribly alive, filled with a mysterium tremendum whose force practically takes away the breath. And then . . . . the silence.

To know love without grasping. To know beauty without wishing ownership. To touch the essence of life within the display of forms is the purpose and meaning of human life. It is in this act that we fulfill our being obligation debt. It is in this profound alchemy of perception that gross matter is transformed into the achingly tender love play of divinity revealed. In this revelation all appearance is redeemed.

Eye to form is only love and this redeems the world.

OTHER TITLES OF INTEREST FROM HOHM PRESS

AS IT IS
A Year on the Road with a Tantric Teacher
by M. Young

A first-hand account of a one-year journey around the world in the company of a *tantric* teacher. This book catalogues the trials and wonders of day-to-day interactions between Western Baul master Lee Lozowick and his students, and presents a broad range of his teachings given in seminars from San Francisco, California to Rishikesh, India. *As It Is* considers the core principles of *tantra*, including non-duality, compassion (the Bodhisattva ideal), service to others, and transformation within daily life. Written as a narrative, this captivating book will appeal to practitioners of *any* spiritual path. Readers interested in a life of clarity, genuine creativity, wisdom and harmony will find this an invaluable resource.

Paper, 725 pages, 24 b&w photos, $29.95   ISBN: 978-0-934252-99-7

• • •

ENLIGHTENED DUALITY
Essays on Art, Beauty, Life and Reality As It Is
by Lee Lozowick and M. Young

This book of essays presents the essential teachings of the Western Baul spiritual master Lee Lozowick, with special emphasis on what he has named "Enlightened Duality." This dynamic spiritual principle suggests that one can combine a firmly-rooted and integrated awareness of the nondual ("all is One") nature of reality, with a lively, conscious relationship to the "duality" or play of opposites that characterizes our everyday lives. Unlike those strictly nondual perspectives that claim a "oneness" that relegates the human experience to an illusion of mind, Lozowick asserts that "unity is the law" *and* "Life is Real." Because this integration of spiritual principles into the whirl of daily relational life is often so challenging, a student's perspective is offered throughout the book, in commentaries by M. Young, a longtime apprentice of Lozowick's.

Paper, 608 pages, 4 color and b&w   ISBN: 978-1-935387-02-2
photos, $24.95

Visit our website at: www.hohmpress.com

OTHER TITLES OF INTEREST FROM HOHM PRESS

JOURNEY TO HEAVENLY MOUNTAIN
An American's Pilgrimage to the Heart of Buddhism in Modern China
by Jay Martin

"I came to China to live in Buddhist monasteries and to revisit my soul," writes best-selling American author and distinguished scholar Jay Martin of his 1998 pilgrimage. This book is an account of one man's spiritual journey. His intention? To penetrate the soul of China and its wisdom. *Journey to Heavenly Mountain* is about the author's desire to know God and sacred things; his yearning for illuminated insight and his hunger to achieve virtue and calmness of spirit. Martin focuses on the profound richness and varieties of inner life, along with the potential for growth in wisdom and empathy which life among these dedicated Buddhists offered.

"Well-written and intelligent, it will appeal to both casual readers and to specialists." —**Library Journal**

Paper, 264 pages, $16.95   ISBN: 978-1-1-890772-17-8

• • •

THE ANTI-WISDOM MANUAL
A Practical Guide to Spiritual Bankruptcy
by Gilles Farcet, Ph.D.

What if the spiritual path turned out to be a road to hell paved with good intentions? Most spiritual books tell us what we *should* do, or how we *should* view things. *The Anti-Wisdom Manual* takes a different approach. It simply describes what people *actually do* to sabotage their own progress on the spiritual path, whatever their chosen way— Christian, Buddhist, Native American, Muslim, Jewish, or any other. Think of it as a handbook in reverse. Using humor and irony, while based in clarity and compassion, the author alerts readers to the common traps into which so many sincere seekers easily fall.

Paper, 176 pages, $14.95   ISBN: 978-1-890772-42-0

Visit our website at: www.hohmpress.com

OTHER TITLES OF INTEREST FROM HOHM PRESS

MUSHOTOKU MIND
The Heart of the Heart Sutra
by Taisen Deshimaru
Revised and Reedited by Richard Collins

Mushotoku mind means an attitude of no profit, no gain. It is the core of Taisen Deshimaru's Zen. This respected master, the head of Japanese Soto Zen for all of Europe, moved from Japan in 1967 and brought this work to Paris, from where it was disseminated throughout the West. This book presents his brilliant commentary on the most renowned of Buddhist texts, the *Heart Sutra*, known in Japanese as *Hannya Shingyo*—a philosophical investigation on *the futility of philosophical investigation*. Deshimaru's work fills a great gap in the interpretations of this seminal text in that he emphasizes "mind-emptiness" (*ku*) as the foundation of Zen practice, in contrast to the usual "mindfulness" focus of other Zen approaches. His lectures on this subject are gathered here into one volume by Zen teacher Richard Collins.

Paper, 190 pages, $16.95   ISBN: 978-1-935387-27-5

• • •

ZEN, SIMPLY SITTING
A Zen Monk's Commentary on the *Fukanzazengi* by Master Dogen
by Philippe Coupey

No diluted, dumbed-down or sugarcoated version of Zen teaching and practice will be found here. Long-time Zen teacher Philippe Coupey offers readers a fresh, sometimes irreverent perspective of an ancient classic, the *Fukanzazengi*, a short basic text on how to practice zazen written by Master Dogen in 1227. Coupey's approach to this timeless teaching is based on the work of his own distinguished master, Taisen Deshimaru, the Japanese Soto Zen teacher who brought Zen to Europe.

Paper, 120 pages, $14.95   ISBN: 978-1-890772-61-1

OTHER TITLES OF INTEREST FROM HOHM PRESS

FEAST OR FAMINE
Teaching on Mind and Emotions
by Lee Lozowick

This book focuses on core issues related to human suffering: the mind that doesn't "Know Thyself," and the emotions that create terrifying imbalance and unhappiness. The author, a spiritual teacher for over 35 years, details the working of mind and emotions, offering practical interventions for when they are raging out of control. A practical handbook for meditators and anyone dedicated to "work on self." Lee Lozowick has written over twenty books, including: *Conscious Parenting; The Alchemy of Transformation;* and *The Alchemy of Love and Sex*; and has been translated and published in French, German, Spanish, Portuguese and other languages.

Paper, 256 pages, $19.95   ISBN: 978-1-890772-79-6

• • •

SELF OBSERVATION ~ THE AWAKENING OF CONSCIENCE
An Owner's Manual
by Red Hawk

This book is an in-depth examination of the much needed process of "self" study known as self observation. It offers the most direct, non-pharmaceutical means of healing the attention dysfunction which plagues contemporary culture. Self observation, the author asserts, is the most ancient, scientific, and proven means to develop conscience, this crucial inner guide to awakening and a moral life.

This book is for the lay-reader, both the beginner and the advanced student of self observation. No other book on the market examines this practice in such detail. There are hundreds of books on self-help and meditation, but almost none on self-study via self observation, and none with the depth of analysis, wealth of explication, and richness of experience that this book offers.

Paper, 160 pages, $14.95   ISBN: 978-1-890772-92-5

OTHER TITLES OF INTEREST FROM HOHM PRESS

WRECKAGE WITH A BEATING HEART
Poems by RedHawk

Red Hawk's poetry has long been acclaimed by his fellow poets, Pulitzer Prize winners and National Book Award Finalists, for its gutsy honesty, plain language, and consummate skill. Never is that poetic skill in rendering the truth more evident than in this, his fifth book of poetry. This collection contains a series of sonnets, some of which he has been working on for thirty years.

Paper, 300 pages, $16.95   ISBN: 978-1-890772-50-5

•••

NOBODY SON OF NOBODY
Poems of Shaikh Abu-Saeed Abhil-Kheir
Renditions by Vraje Abramian

Anyone who has found a resonance with the love-intoxicated poetry of Rumi will profit from the poetry of Shaikh Abil-Kheir. This renowned but little known Sufi mystic of the 10th century preceded Rumi by over two hundred years on the same path of annihilation into God. This book contains translations and poetic renderings of 195 short selections from the original Farsi, the language in which Abil-Kheir wrote.

These poems deal with the longing for union with God, the desire to know the Real from the false, the inexpressible beauty of creation when seen through the eyes of Love, and the many attitudes of heart, mind and feeling that are necessary to those who would find the Beloved, The Friend, in this life.

Paper, 104 pages, $12.95   ISBN: 978-1-890772-08-6

Visit our website at: www.hohmpress.com

OTHER TITLES OF INTEREST FROM HOHM PRESS

THE JUMP INTO LIFE
Moving Beyond Fear
by Arnaud Desjardins
Foreword by Richard Moss, M.D.

"Say Yes to life," the author continually invites in this welcome guidebook to the spiritual path. For anyone who has ever felt oppressed by the life-negative seriousness of religion, this book is a timely antidote. In language that translates the complex to the obvious, Desjardins applies his simple teaching of happiness and gratitude to a broad range of weighty topics, including sexuality and intimate relationships, structuring an "inner life," the relief of suffering, and overcoming fear.

Paper, 216 pages, $12.95   ISBN: 978-0-934252-42-3

• • •

THE MIRROR OF THE SKY
Songs of the Bauls of Bengal
Translated by Deben Bhattacharya

Baul music today is prized by world musicologists, and Baul lyrics are treasured by readers of ecstatic and mystical poetry. Their music, lyrics and accompanying dance reflect the passion, the devotion and the iconoclastic freedom of this remarkable sect of musicians and lovers of the Divine, affectionately known as "God's troubadours." The Mirror of the Sky is a translation of 204 songs, including an extensive introduction to the history and faith of the Bauls, and the composition of their music. It includes a CD of authentic Baul artists, recorded as much as forty years ago by Bhattacharya, a specialist in world music. The current CD is a rare presentation of this infrequently documented genre.

Paper, 288 pages, $24.95 (includes CD)   ISBN: 978-0-934252-89-8
CD sold separately, $16.95

Visit our website at: www.hohmpress.com

OTHER TITLES OF INTEREST FROM HOHM PRESS

YOGI RAMSURATKUMAR: **Under the Punnai Tree**
by M. Young

Hohm Press's first full-length biography of the wondrous and blessed beggar of Tiruvannamalai. More than 80 photographs. To be touched by the truth, beauty and love of this remarkable being will stir the heart's deepest longings. This book celebrates the inspiration of one rare individual who abandoned everything for the love of God.

Paper, 752 pages, $39.95   ISBN: 978-1-890772-34-5

• • •

ONLY GOD: **A Biography of Yogi Ramsuratkumar**
by Regina Sara Ryan

"Only God" was the Yogi's creed and approach to life. His unusual innocence and radiant presence were recognized by seekers from East and West. This book includes the lives and teachings of the holy beggar's three gurus: Ramana Maharshi, Sri Aurobindo, and Swami Papa Ramdas. An enjoyable mix of storytelling, interviews and fact finding.

Hardcover, 832 pages, $39.95   ISBN: 978-1-890772-35-2

• • •

A MAN AND HIS MASTER: **My Years with Yogi Ramsuratkumar**
by Mani, with S. Lkasham

Yogi Ramsuratkumar is unique, even in India's long and rich tradition—and Mani was his closest servant, his trusted "right-hand man." Mani's heart and devotion shine through this touchingly personal account of his six years at the Master's side.

Paper, 394 pages, $21.95   ISBN: 978-1-890772-36-9

OTHER TITLES OF INTEREST FROM HOHM PRESS

FATHER AND SON: The Indian Beggar King Yogi Ramsuratkumar and the American Master and Bad Poet Lee Lozowick
by V.J. Fedorschak

A contemporary spiritual epic of the traditional Guru-devotee relationship. This book chronicles the twenty-six years (1976-2001) of exchange between Lee Lozowick and his Master. Contains numerous interviews and color photos.

Hardcover, 992 pages, $89.95   ISBN: 978-1-890772-84-0

• • •

THE REVOLUTION FROM WITHIN
by J. Krishnamurti

"There must be a revolution in our thinking," declares the author, J. Krishnamurti (1895-1986), who remains one of the greatest philosophers and teachers of modern times. In this series of lectures, given in the U.S. and various cities throughout the world in the 1950s, he again confronts the habitual, projection-making mind, which fails to see *what is* while it absorbs itself in belief and illusion. Topics covered in these essays include: the process of change at all levels; the development of discipline; quieting the mind; self-awareness; and freedom from slavery to mind. Krishnamurti explains that only by rigorous self-observation and self-questioning is there any hope that humankind will overcome its blindness and self-obsession enough to bring about an end of violence, war and other misery on this beleaguered planet.

Paper, 320 pages, + DVD, $19.95   ISBN: 978-1-935387-05-3

Visit our website at: www.hohmpress.com

OTHER TITLES OF INTEREST FROM HOHM PRESS

AS ONE IS
To Free the Mind from All Conditioning
by J. Krishnamurti

In this series of previously unpublished lectures, Krishnamurti examines a world in which booming productivity and scientific advancement *should* promise a happy future, but don't. He asks his listeners to consider that we are merely substituting comfortable myths for our fears, and living as if these myths were true. The author patiently explains how to examine our assumptions; how to question our "conditioned" beliefs, and ultimately how to listen for truth... both within and from the world around us. *As One Is* offers readers a rare opportunity to gain greater self-understanding, and clarity in the midst of confusion. Krishnamurti offers a means to transform thinking and hence our relationship to life.

"I know of no other living man whose thought is more inspiring."
— Henry Miller

Paper, 120 pages, $14.95   ISBN: 978-1-890772-62-8

• • •

ZEN TRASH
The Irreverent and Sacred Teaching Stories of Lee Lozowick
Edited and with Commentary by Sylvan Incao

This book contains dozens of teaching stories from many world religious traditions—including Zen, Christianity, Tibetan Buddhism, Sufism and Hinduism—rendered with a twist of humor, irony or provocation by contemporary Western Baul spiritual teacher Lee Lozowick. They are compiled from twenty-five years of Lozowick's talks and seminars in the U.S., Canada, Europe, Mexico and India. These stories will typically confound the mind and challenge any conventional seriousness about the spiritual path. In essence, however, they hold what every traditional teaching story has always held—the possibility of glimpsing reality, beyond the multiple illusions that surround the truth.

Paper, 156 pages, $12. 95   ISBN: 978-1-890772-21-5

Visit our website at: www.hohmpress.com

OTHER TITLES OF INTEREST FROM HOHM PRESS

CAUGHT IN THE BELOVED'S PETTICOATS
A Treatise on the Eternal Way
by M. Young

Written in the style of a wayfarer's journal, this book chronicles the travels and teachings of Western Baul Master, Lee Lozowick, during the summer of 2005, which marked thirty years since the commencement of his teaching work. From the Southwestern desert of the U.S. to England, France and Germany, readers join the caravan of travelers with the spiritual Master, meeting him and his students in unexpected situations, both usual and extraordinary, and sharing in the insight, provocation, art, music, grace and grit in which this living teacher offers up gems of wisdom with eloquence, humor and honesty.

Paper, 692 pages, $35.00   ISBN: 978-1-890772-63-5

• • •

FACETS OF THE DIAMOND
Wisdom of India
by James Capellini

A book of rare and moving photographs, brief biographies, and evocative quotes from contemporary spiritual teachers in the Eastern tradition, including Ramana Maharshi, Swami Papa Ramdas, Sri Yogi Ramsuratkumar, Swami Prajnanpad, Chandra Swami, Nityananda, Shirdi Sai Baba, and Sanatan Das Baul. This mood-altering book richly captures the texture and flavor of the Eastern spiritual path and the teacher-disciple relationship, and offers penetrating insight into the lives of those who carry the flame of wisdom for the good of all humanity.

Hardcover, 240 pages, $39.95,   ISBN: 978-0-934252-53-9
45 b&w photographs

OTHER TITLES OF INTEREST FROM HOHM PRESS

THE YOGA TRADITION
Its History, Literature, Philosophy and Practice
by Georg Feuerstein, Ph.D.
New Foreword by Subhash Kak, Ph.D.

A complete overview of the great Yogic traditions of: Raja-Yoga, Hatha-Yoga, Jnana-Yoga, Bhakti-Yoga, Karma-Yoga, Tantra-Yoga, Kundalini-Yoga, Mantra-Yoga and many other lesser known forms. Includes translations of over twenty famous Yoga treatises, like the *Yoga-Sutra* of Patanjali, and a first-time translation of the *Goraksha Paddhati*, an ancient Hatha Yoga text. Covers all aspects of Hindu, Buddhist, Jaina and Sikh Yoga. A necessary resource for all students and scholars of Yoga.

Paper, 520 pages, $29.95,   ISBN: 978-1-890772-18-5
over 200 illustrations

• • •

IGNITING THE INNER LIFE
by Regina Sara Ryan

This book will serve as a welcome friend to any pilgrim who wants to move deeper within. It will encourage long term but weary travelers to take that next step, and point out common detours or dead ends along this interior highway. Each chapter contains one or more contemporary poems to uplift the reader. The book concludes with suggested practices and prayers to rekindle the heart's intentions. *Igniting the Inner Life* is directed to those with a focus on spirituality, self-understanding, contemplative prayer, God, or the awakening of the heart's knowledge, regardless of the religious tradition they follow.

Paper, 192 pages, $16.95   ISBN: 978-1-935387-17-6

Visit our website at: www.hohmpress.com

About the Author

TRAKTUNG YESHE DORJE is an American born spiritual teacher who has taught in the U.S., Cuba, and Europe since 1990. For twenty-two years he has guided the Tsogyelgar spiritual community outside Ann Arbor, Michigan. His root guru—Lama Thinley Norbu Rinpoche—encouraged him to write so as to clarify Vajrayana Buddhism for western audiences. He has guided the creation of America's largest mural of Tantric art, and overseen the creation of a Western form of *doha* songs (celebrations of spiritual teaching), now on several CDs. He is president of Wishing Tree Gardens, a non-profit sustainable-agriculture educational program.

Contact Information: Traktung Yeshe Dorje, *www.traktung.org*

About Hohm Press

HOHM PRESS is committed to publishing books that provide readers with alternatives to the materialistic values of the current culture, and promote self-awareness, the recognition of interdependence, and compassion. Our subject areas include parenting, transpersonal psychology, religious studies, women's studies, the arts and poetry.

Contact Information: Hohm Press, PO Box 4410, Chino Valley, Arizona, 86323; USA; 800-381-2700, or 928-636-3331; email: *hppublisher@cableone.net*

Visit our website at *www.hohmpress.com*